Concise
Ga
Wil
Guide

There are 47 individual Wildlife Trusts covering the whole of the UK and the Isle of Man and Alderney. Together The Wildlife Trusts are the largest UK voluntary organization dedicated to protecting wildlife and wild places everywhere – at land and sea. They are supported by 791,000 members, 150,000 of whom belong to their junior branch, Wildlife Watch. Every year The Wildlife Trusts work with thousands of schools, and their nature reserves and visitor centres receive millions of visitors.

The Wildlife Trusts work in partnership with hundreds of landowners and businesses across the UK in towns, cities and the wider countryside. Building on their existing network of 2,250 nature reserves, The Wildlife Trusts' recovery plan for the UK's wildlife and fragmented habitats, known as A Living Landscape, is being achieved through restoring, recreating and reconnecting large areas of wildlife habitat. As well as protecting wildlife this is helping to safeguard the ecosystems that we depend on for services like clean air and water.

The Wildlife Trusts are also working to protect the UK's marine environment. They are involved with many marine conservation projects around the UK, often surveying and collecting vital data on the state of our seas. Every year they run National Marine Week in August – a two-week celebration of our seas with hundreds of events taking place around the UK.

All 47 Wildlife Trusts are members of the Royal Society of Wildlife Trusts (Registered charity number 207238). To find your local Wildlife Trust visit wildlifetrusts.org

BLOOMSBURY

Concise

# Garden Wildlife

Guide

BLOOMSBURY WILDLIFE
LONDON • OXFORD • NEW YORK • NEW DELHI • SYDNEY

BLOOMSBURY WILDLIFE
Bloomsbury Publishing Plc
50 Bedford Square, London, WC1B 3DP, UK

BLOOMSBURY, BLOOMSBURY WILDLIFE and the Diana logo are trademarks of
Bloomsbury Publishing Plc

First published in 2011 by New Holland Publishers (UK) Ltd
This edition published in 2015 by Bloomsbury Publishing Plc

A catalogue record for this book is available from the British Library

ISBN: PB: 978-1-4729-6664-3; ePub: 978-1-4729-1982-3; ePDF: 978-1-4729-1981-6

2 4 6 8 10 9 7 5 3 1

Printed in China by Leo Paper Products

Design by Alan Marshall

The publishers thank Shirley Hawkins of the Wildlife Trusts for reading the text

To find out more about our authors and books visit www.bloomsbury.com
and sign up for our newsletters

# Contents

# Introduction

Gardens in northern Europe are wonderful places to start watching wildlife, and even the smallest garden can support a variety of animals, from snails and spiders, to birds and small mammals. So many species can turn up in a garden that this book cannot include them all. It will, however, give you a good idea of the animals that can be found in your garden, and help you to identify them.

Although gardens are somewhat artificial as environments, they usually have obvious traces of the habitat that they have replaced. Where houses have been built in what was once woodland, a garden may, for example, contain a mature oak tree, which attracts bird and insect species not found in other gardens. Where they have been built on farmland, there may be the remnants of hedges with their characteristic woodland edge fauna.

## Food & Behaviour

Food, shelter and reproduction are the keys to an animal's survival, and are important factors in identifying the species. Some of the animals that come into gardens may be unwelcome because they eat the plants grown by gardeners, while others should be encouraged because they feed on pest species and provide some control over their numbers.

Animals occur at different seasons. The Swallow, for example, appears in March–April, and disappears in September–October, because it is a migrant. It breeds in continental Europe, and when the insects it eats become scarce, it flies south for the winter. Other birds change their habits to cope with the changes of food from season to season. Blackbirds concentrate on earthworms, insects and other invertebrates when they are plentiful in summer, but turn to berries and fruits in autumn and winter. It is in winter, when food is scarce, that birds are attracted most to gardens.

The life cycle of all insects includes a number of stages, which take an insect throughout the year from egg to adult insect. The Peacock, a common garden butterfly, is first seen as the weather warms in March and it emerges from hibernation to breed. After May it seems to disappear, because the adults have bred and the new generation is going from eggs to larvae to pupae, to finally emerge as butterflies in July–September. On sunny days they can be seen feeding on the nectar of the last Michaelmas Daisies or the juices of rotting windfall fruits, before hibernating throughout the winter. In the depths of winter you might come across one in a corner of the garden shed or even in the house (do not disturb it if you do).

Reproduction is, of course, an essential part of the lives of all animals. Birds sing in spring to proclaim that they hold a territory and to attract a mate. The flight of male Brimstone butterflies on warm spring mornings has the same purpose. You may notice other butterflies – as well as dragonflies – patrolling your garden in search of a mate. Having paired, birds find places in which to build nests and rear young, and there has to be sufficient food for their offspring. Insects have to find the foodplants on which their larvae can feed or, if they are predatory, enough of their prey.

## Making a Garden Fit for Wildlife

If you garden in a non-harmful organic way, avoiding using herbicides and pesticides, you will attract wildlife, even though you may have a conventional short-cut lawn and formal herbaceous borders. During the breeding season, try to minimize disturbance to hedges and places where birds nest, and to compost heaps, which provide refuge for a host of wildlife from Hedgehogs and Grass Snakes, to earthworms and centipedes. Discourage cats, which are the greatest killers of garden wildlife.

## Attracting Wildlife

Birds can be enticed to the smallest garden by putting out *food* such as kitchen scraps and seeds. They are also attracted by berry-bearing shrubs. Insects like bees, hoverflies and butterflies can be lured by planting bushes and flowering plants from which they can extract nectar and pollen.

Shelter in the form of *nestboxes* attracts birds, but they will only nest if there is sufficient food in the form of small insects available, because even the seed-eating species feed their young on insects. Many insects and other invertebrates require shelter when they are not active, and if you look under leaf litter, logs and stones you will find them in large numbers. *Hollow sticks* held into a frame with chicken wire can provide holes in which solitary bees and wasps can nest. *Compost heaps*, as well as constituting a positive way of reusing waste, are important as places for invertebrates to live and breed in. They may also provide hibernation places for Hedgehogs, Grass Snakes and toads. A *pond* attracts frogs, toads, newts and aquatic insects, and provides birds and mammals with somewhere to drink and bathe.

# Common Earthworm
## *Lumbricus terrestris*

SIZE AND DESCRIPTION Length
90–300mm. Bright pink to reddish-
brown, sometimes with a violet tinge.
Consists of about 150 segments with
a reddish-orange citellum on segments
33–36. (The citellum is the armband-like
swollen part on a fully grown worm's body,
which produces cocoons in which the worm's
embryos develop.) The largest of about 10
earthworm species found in British gardens.

HABITAT Occurs across most of Europe in any soil that is not
too wet or too acid.

FOOD AND HABITS Swallows soil and digests any organic material
that it needs, expelling the rest.

▼ SIMILAR SPECIES **Angler's Red Worm** (*L. rubellus*). 25–140mm long.
Bright red-brown with a citellum on segments 28–31. Habitat
and feeding as for Common Earthworm.

# Blue-grey Worm
*Octolasion cyaneum*

Length 40–180mm. Greyish-blue with a red citellum on segments 29–33 or 30–34. There are 150–165 body segments. Yellowish tail. Widespread in moist soils throughout Europe. Feeds beneath the soil on decaying material. Emits a thick milky fluid when disturbed.

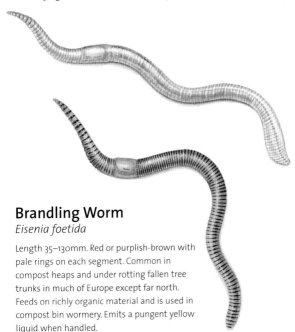

# Brandling Worm
*Eisenia foetida*

Length 35–130mm. Red or purplish-brown with pale rings on each segment. Common in compost heaps and under rotting fallen tree trunks in much of Europe except far north. Feeds on richly organic material and is used in compost bin wormery. Emits a pungent yellow liquid when handled.

# Chestnut Worm
*Lumbricius castaneus*

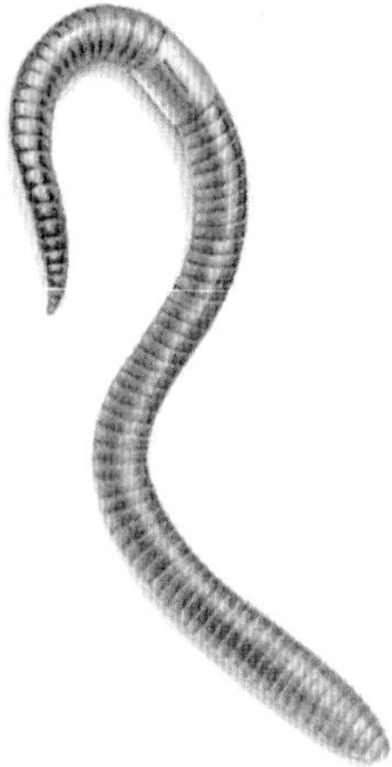

Length 30–70mm. Brown with
a bright orange clitellum on
segments 29–32. Widespread in
Europe where soil is suitable.
Absent from Spain and Portugal.
Behaviour similar to that of
Common Earthworm (page 8).

# Turgid Worm
*Allolobophora nocturna*

Length 90–180mm. Dark reddish-brown
becoming purplish towards the rear end. Body has
200–246 segments. Found across most of Europe in any
soil that is not too wet or too acid. Not as widespread as Long Worm
(opposite). Swallows soil and digests organic material. Nocturnal.

# Long Worm
*Allolobophora longa*

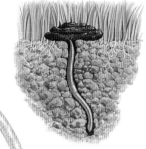

**How worm casts
are formed**

SIZE AND DESCRIPTION Length 90–170mm.
Clitellum covers 8–9 segments between
segments 27–36. Body has 170–190 segments.
HABITAT Widespread throughout Europe in gardens, on
cultivated land and in woodland, on chalky or loamy soil.
FOOD AND HABITS Swallows soil, taking from it what it needs,
and expelling the rest in the form of worm casts, which are
often visible on the surface. In doing so it breaks up the soil,
and helps to make it more fertile.

# Thunderworm
*Mermis nigrescens*

Length to 50 cm. Looks like a piece of brown or white cotton. Body not segmented. Occurs in soils across Europe, but more common in south than in north. Lives in soil, but emerges after rain and twines itself around low-growing plants. Female lays eggs on plants, which are eaten by insects. Young worms hatch inside insect and feed on its fluids, emerging on maturity to live in soil. Host is weakened but not necessarily killed.

# Earthworm
*Octolasion lacteum*

Length 25–160mm. Bluish with an orange or pink clitellum on segments 30–35. Body has 100–135 segments. Found under stones and logs, decaying leaves and compost in pasture, arable land and gardens. Widespread in southern and western Europe. Feeds beneath soil on decaying material.

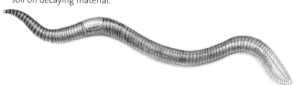

# Potato Root Eelworm
## *Globodera rostochensis*

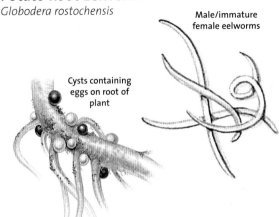

**Cysts containing eggs on root of plant**

**Male/immature female eelworms**

**SIZE AND DESCRIPTION** Length to 30mm. Whitish nematode (roundworm). Males and juveniles of both sexes are mobile and threadlike. Also called Cyst Nematode and Root Nematode.

**HABITAT** Farmland and gardens where potatoes are grown. Probably originated in Peru.

**FOOD AND HABITS** After fertilization, females transform into spherical cysts 0.1–0.8mm across. This happens when the eggs develop and cause the body of the female to swell. She then becomes a cyst and dies. Each cyst contains 200–1,000 eggs, which can survive for up to 20 years in the cysts. New cysts are glossy brown and rounded; they pass through a yellow stage before rupturing. Hatching is favoured by humidity and a substance secreted by the host plant.

# Rounded Snail
*Discus rotundatus*

**SIZE AND DESCRIPTION** Shell diameter to 6mm. A disk snail with a pale yellow-brown shell that has broad reddish stripes. Body is grey.

**HABITAT** Found everywhere except in the driest habitats. Very common in leaf litter and in garden compost heaps.

**FOOD AND HABITS** Feeds on decaying plant material and fungi.

# Brown-lipped Snail
## *Cepaea nemoralis*

**Size and description** Shell diameter 18 x 22mm. Lip of shell usually brown, sometimes very pale. Shell colour straw to yellow, to pink to brown. Up to five dark spiral bands, but sometimes none.

**Habitat** Inhabits woods, hedges, rough vegetation and gardens (but less frequently than White-lipped Snail). Found across Europe, but not as far north as White-lipped Snail.

**Food and habits** Eats grass and low-growing plants. Feeds at night and after rain, often alongside other species.

▼ **Similar species White-lipped Snail** (*C. hortensis*). Shell diameter 14 x 17mm. Lip of shell is usually white, sometimes brown. Shell has up to five dark spirals, but may have none. Found in woods, hedges and gardens, especially in moist habitats. Occurs throughout Europe as far north as Iceland. Food and habits similar to those of Brown-lipped Snail.

# Strawberry Snail
*Trichia striolata*

SIZE AND DESCRIPTION  Shell diameter 14mm. Colour of flattened-spiral shell varies from yellow to reddish-brown or purple, with a prominent white ring around the shell mouth.

HABITAT  Hedgerows, gardens and wasteland with plenty of moisture. Occurs from Britain across Europe to Hungary.

FOOD AND HABITS  Mainly nocturnal, but also browses on plants after rain. Shelters under plants during the day.

# Garden Snail
*Helix aspersa*

**SIZE AND DESCRIPTION** Shell diameter 25–40mm. Large round shell with a wide, round white-lipped mouth. Shell is brown or yellowish with pale flecking and up to five darker spirals.

**HABITAT** Parks, woods and wasteland throughout Europe. Frequently found in gardens, especially in northern regions, where it needs shelter from the winter cold.

**FOOD AND HABITS** Feeds on low-growing plants. Active at night, and congregates during the day at regular resting places.

# Kentish Snail
*Monacha cantiana*

**SIZE AND DESCRIPTION** Shell diameter to 20mm. Shell colour varies from off-white to reddish-pink, and is often darker near the mouth.
**HABITAT** Long grass in hedge banks, wasteland, fields and herbaceous garden borders on calcareous soils. Widespread throughout southern and central Europe.
**FOOD AND HABITS** Feeds on decaying vegetation, including lawn grass cuttings.

# Great Pond Snail
*Lymnaea stagnalis*

**SIZE AND DESCRIPTION** Shell height 35–50mm; width 18–25mm. Pointed spiral shell is yellowish to dark brown.
**HABITAT** Large calcium-rich ponds, and slow-flowing rivers and canals. Widely distributed across Europe, and common in many countries.
**FOOD AND HABITS** Feeds on algae and decaying vegetation. Eggs are laid in a sausage-shaped gelatinous sac on the undersides of leaves.

# Garlic Snail
*Oxychilus alliarius*

**SIZE AND DESCRIPTION** Shell diameter 6mm. A species of glass snail with a dark brown shell that is very glossy. Body is black. When disturbed it gives off a strong smell similar to that of garlic or onions, hence its common name.

**HABITAT** Found in leaf litter in a range of habitats. Lurks under stones and in garden compost heaps.

**FOOD AND HABITS** Feeds mainly at night on fungi and rotting vegetation on the ground, but also climbs walls and trees on damp nights.

# Great Ram's-horn Snail
*Planorbis corneus*

**SIZE AND DESCRIPTION** Shell diameter up to 35mm; height 12mm. The shape of the dark brown shell gives this large snail its common name.
**HABITAT** Ponds, lakes and slow-flowing rivers. Also found in garden ponds because it is sold by aquarium dealers. Native range is from Europe to central Asia.
**FOOD AND HABITS** Feeds on algae on stones and plants. Its eggs, which are laid on stones, may be spread to other ponds whenever they stick to the feet of birds.

# Garden Slug
*Arion hortensis*

**SIZE AND DESCRIPTION** Length to 40mm. Bluish-black and paler on flanks, with an orange underside. Mucus is orange or yellow.
**HABITAT** Most common on cultivated land, but can also be found in woods and gardens. Occurs throughout Europe except far north.
**FOOD AND HABITS** Eats any plants near the ground, and is a serious pest of strawberries, lettuces and seedlings.
▼ **SIMILAR SPECIES Bourguignat's Slug** (*A. fasciatus*). To 40mm long. Body grey with dark patches. Similar to Garden Slug, but with a white underside. Found in gardens and woods. Feeds on fungi and decaying material.

# Large Black Slug
*Arion ater*

**SIZE AND DESCRIPTION** Length to 150mm; may reach 200mm when extended. Colour ranges from jet-black through orange, to creamy-white with an orange fringe. Back is covered with elongated tubercles. No keel. Sticky mucus.

**HABITAT** Well-vegetated habitats throughout Europe to Iceland. Darker forms are most common in north, paler ones in south.

**FOOD AND HABITS** Nocturnal feeder on dung, plants and carrion. Eats grass cuttings after rain.

# Great Grey Slug
## *Limax maximus*

Length to 200mm. Pale grey slug heavily marked with dark spots, appearing striped at the end of its body. Short keel on the rear end of the body. Inhabits woods, hedges and gardens, especially around compost heaps, in much of Europe except far north. Eats fungi and rotting plant material. Mating involves two individuals climbing a fence, tree trunk or wall, then lowering themselves on a string of mucus. Each of these hermaphrodites then lays eggs.

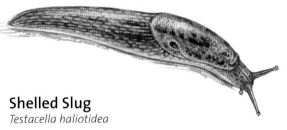

# Shelled Slug
## *Testacella haliotidea*

Length to 120mm. Creamy-white or pale yellow body, with a small flat shell at the rear end. Dark lines run forwards at angles along the sides of the body. Lives in well-manured and well-drained soil in parks and gardens across western Europe. Main food is earthworms. It can extend its body to become narrow enough to follow worms down their holes.

# Netted Slug
*Deroceras reticulatum*

Length to 50mm. Small in size. Light brown or dark grey with darker flecks and rectangular tubercles that create a netted pattern. Short keel at the rear. Occurs in gardens, hedges, arable fields and rough pasture. One of Europe's most common and most widespread slugs. Exudes white mucus when disturbed. Eats a wide range of plants, especially newly planted seedlings, and is regarded as a garden pest.

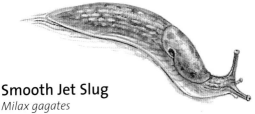

# Smooth Jet Slug
*Milax gagates*

Length to 75mm. Greyish-brown and heavily specked, with a keel darker than the rest of its body. Exudes clear mucus. Very similar to Sowerby's Slug (*M. sowerbyi*), which has a yellowish or orange keel and exudes yellowish mucus. Relatively dry-skinned. Inhabits gardens and arable fields. Most common in western Europe. Feeds on roots and tubers.

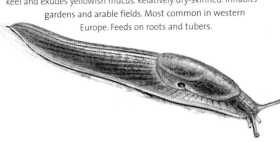

# Spotted Snake Millipede
*Blaniulus guttulatus*

**SIZE AND DESCRIPTION** Length 15mm; diameter to 0.7mm. Pale with red spots on either flank. The spots are glands that release a repellent liquid, which acts as a defence against predators.

**HABITAT** Arable fields and gardens on heavy damp soils across Europe.

**FOOD AND HABITS** Burrows and eats rotting material, but feeds on roots in dry weather. Millipedes are mostly vegetarian, unlike centipedes, and move relatively slowly. This is one of about 50 millipede species found in Britain.

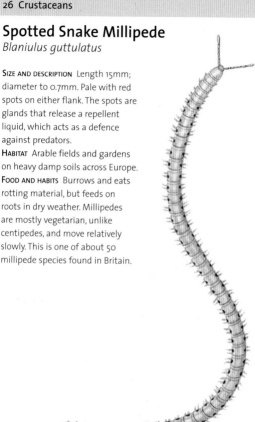

# Flat-backed Millipede
*Polydesmus angustus*

Length to 25mm; width to 4mm. Looks like
a centipede, but has two pairs of legs on
each segement. Flattened body segments
are equipped with about 20 pairs of legs.
Lives in leaf litter, turf, organically rich soils
and garden compost heaps across most of
Europe. Eats decaying vegetation, but
also nibbles plant roots and soft fruits,
including strawberries.

# Greenhouse Millipede
*Oxidus gracilis*

Length to 23mm; width to 2.5mm.
Resembles Flat-backed Millipede
(above), but has a smoother and more
rounded back. There are two pairs of
legs on each body segment. A tropical
species that has become established
in European greenhouses. Feeds on
decayed and living plant matter. Lays
eggs throughout the year.

# Snake Millipede
*Tachypodiulus niger*

Length to 50mm; diameter to 4mm. Cylindrical shiny black-brown body that tapers at each end. Inhabits hedges, garden borders and woodland in much of Europe. Lives in the surface layer of soil, under loose bark and in leaf litter. Feeds at night on living and decaying plants. Climbs Raspberry canes to reach fruits. Coils up when disturbed.

# Black Millipede
*Cylindroiulus londinensis*

Length to 50mm; diameter to 4mm. Shiny black body, slightly less tapering at each end than that of Snake Millipede. Also called White-legged Snake Millipede. Inhabits the surface layers of soil, loose bark and leaves. Feeds on plant material. Nocturnal.

# Pill Millipede
## *Glomeris marginata*

**SIZE AND DESCRIPTION** Length to 20mm; width to 3mm. There are 17–19 pairs of legs. Often confused with Pill Woodlouse (page 32). They look similar, but Pill Millipede's dorsal plates are shinier and deeper, and it has a broad and almost semi-circular plate at the rear.

**HABITAT** Leaf litter and turf in woodland, hedges and gardens across Europe. Able to endure drier conditions than other millipedes.

**FOOD AND HABITS** Eats stems and dead vegetation. Rolls up into a ball when disturbed.

# Common Woodlouse
*Oniscus asellus*

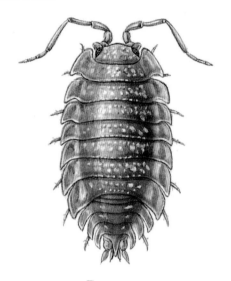

SIZE AND DESCRIPTION Length 15mm; width 8mm. Body sections of this woodlouse are not very obvious, giving it a relatively smooth outline. Shiny grey in colour, with yellow or cream blotches and pale edges to the plates on its back. Looks flatter than other woodlice.

HABITAT Abundant in lime-rich soils across Europe, especially under logs and in compost heaps in gardens. One of the most common garden species.

FOOD AND HABITS Very fond of rotting wood and other plant material. Woodlice shed their skin as they grow.

# Rough Woodlouse
*Porcellio scaber*

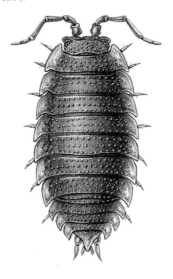

**SIZE AND DESCRIPTION** Length 17mm; width 7mm. Dull grey in colour, with noticeable tubercles and pale spots. Like other woodlice, has 14 legs. One of about 50 woodlice species found in Britain.

**HABITAT** Able to tolerate drier conditions than Common Woodlouse (opposite), with which it is often found beneath logs or under stones. Very common throughout Europe.

**FOOD AND HABITS** Feeds at night on algae on walls and tree trunks.

# Pill Woodlouse
*Armadillidium vulgare*

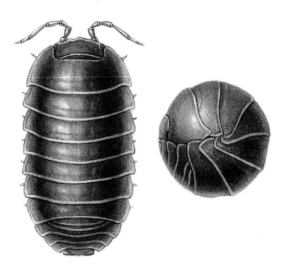

**SIZE AND DESCRIPTION** Length 18mm. Smooth and shiny slate-grey body has a domed back with a tinge of blue, or sometimes brown or yellow.
**HABITAT** Dry grassland, but restricted mainly to lime-rich soils. More tolerant of drier habitats than other woodlouse species. Widely distributed and common in much of Europe except north. Often found at bases of walls.
**FOOD AND HABITS** Rolls itself into a ball, or 'pill', if disturbed. When it is curled up it can be distinguished from Pill Millipede (page 29) by the numerous small plates at its rear.

# Pink Woodlouse
## *Androniscus dentiger*

Length 6mm. Body is pale, sometimes pinkish, usually with a darker central stripe. Prominent spined tubercles cover the body. Large eyes for its size. Also called Rosy Woodlouse. Lives in coastal areas, old quarries and caves where there is a significant amount of lime available. Can be found in compost heaps, leaf litter and cellars. Occurs throughout Europe except far north. Attracted by limestone on walls.

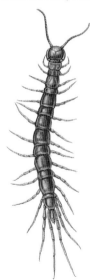

# Common Centipede
## *Lithobius forficatus*

Length 18–30mm; width 4mm. Shiny chestnut-brown. Adults have 15 pairs of legs; hatchlings have 7 pairs, growing extra pairs at each moult. Head is rounded. Centipedes have one pair of legs on each segment, unlike millipedes, which have two pairs per segment. Widespread in Europe, from moorlands to coasts. Abundant in gardens. Hides under stones and logs in daytime. At night it hunts insects, other centipedes, worms and slugs. Centipedes are capable of moving very fast when hunting prey.

# Garden Centipede
*Scutigerella immaculata*

SIZE AND DESCRIPTION Length 7mm.
Long antennae and 12 pairs of
short legs. Very like a true
centipede (hence its inclusion
here with the centipedes), but
in fact part of another group of
arthropods called symphylans.
HABITAT Soil and leaf litter in
several habitats, including
woodland and gardens.
FOOD AND HABITS Feeds mainly
on dead and decaying plant
material, and seedlings.

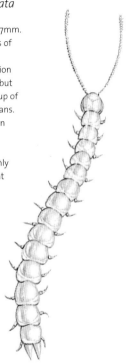

# Soil centipede
*Necrophloeophagus longicornis*

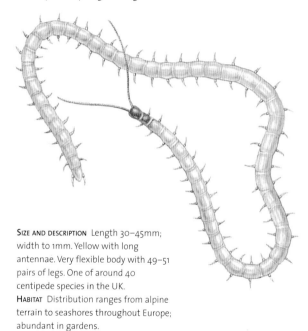

**SIZE AND DESCRIPTION** Length 30–45mm;
width to 1mm. Yellow with long
antennae. Very flexible body with 49–51
pairs of legs. One of around 40
centipede species in the UK.

**HABITAT** Distribution ranges from alpine
terrain to seashores throughout Europe;
abundant in gardens.

**FOOD AND HABITS** A burrowing predator.

# Soil centipede
*Geophilus carpophagus*

SIZE AND DESCRIPTION
Length 40mm (may be
longer); width to 1.5mm.
Reddish-brown body
that is very flexible,
with 45–55 pairs of legs.
**HABITAT** Soil or leaf
matter in woodland,
orchards and gardens
throughout Europe.
Also found in cellars
and damp outbuildings.
**FOOD AND HABITS** A fast-
moving predator that
lives in soil.

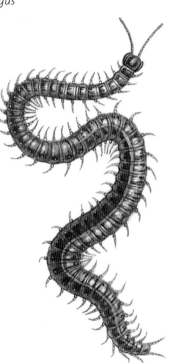

# Soil centipede
*Haplophilus subterraneus*

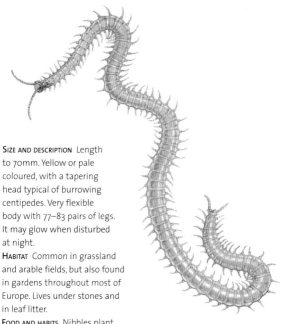

**SIZE AND DESCRIPTION** Length to 70mm. Yellow or pale coloured, with a tapering head typical of burrowing centipedes. Very flexible body with 77–83 pairs of legs. It may glow when disturbed at night.

**HABITAT** Common in grassland and arable fields, but also found in gardens throughout most of Europe. Lives under stones and in leaf litter.

**FOOD AND HABITS** Nibbles plant roots and feeds on small subterranean animals.

# Water Hog-louse
*Ascellus aquaticus*

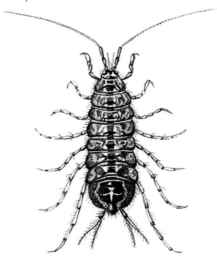

SIZE AND DESCRIPTION Length to 15mm. Grey-brown body that is flattened dorso-ventrally. Seven pairs of walking legs. Very recognizable because it is the closest living relative of woodlice.

HABITAT Widespread and abundant in small stagnant ponds; also found along canal margins and in sluggish streams with weeds and leaf litter.

FOOD AND HABITS Like woodlice it is a recycler, grubbing around in weeds and dead plant matter at the bottoms of ponds. Female lays eggs in April–May, then carries them around in her marsupium (pouch). Young remain in the pouch for a while even after hatching.

# Cyclops
*Cyclops* sp.

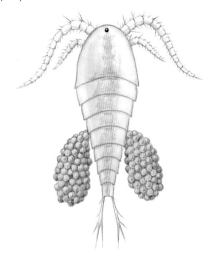

**SIZE AND DESCRIPTION** Length to 3mm. Pear-shaped body ending in a forked tail. Single eye and long antennules (first antennae). There are around 40 species of cyclops in Britain, all of which are very similar.
**HABITAT** Widespread in all kinds of freshwater body apart from the most polluted.
**FOOD AND HABITS** Feeds on food particles suspended in water, and on dead animals. Two egg sacs are carried by female on her side, like large panniers (as shown above). Lives for a year or less.

# Freshwater Shrimp
*Gammarus lacustris*

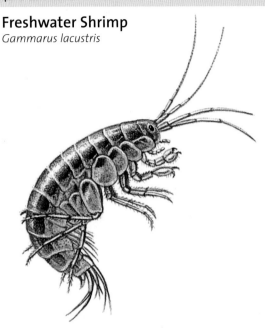

**SIZE AND DESCRIPTION** Length to 25mm. Drab olive, grey-brown or red-brown body that is curved. Antennules are only slightly longer than the antennae. Swims on its side.

**HABITAT** Widespread and often abundant in lakes across northern Britain, Ireland and northern Germany northwards, and also found in ponds.

**FOOD AND HABITS** Scavenges in water, performing the same function as woodlice do above the surface.

# Water Flea
*Daphne pulex*

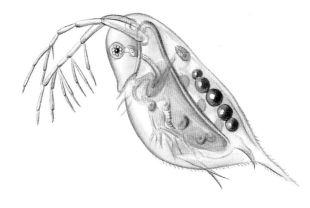

**SIZE AND DESCRIPTION** Length to 5mm. Swims using second pair of antennae (smaller first pair is sensory).
**HABITAT** Shallow weedy ponds, lake edges and debris in still fresh water. Can be abundant, with 'blooms' giving water a red-brown tinge.
**FOOD AND HABITS** Filters food particles from water. Lives from a few weeks to six months.

# Common Darter
*Sympetrum striolatum*

**SIZE AND DESCRIPTION** Length 35–44mm; hindwing 24–30mm. Male is red with a narrow pointed abdomen. Female is greenish-yellow. Thorax and eyes are dark brown in both sexes. Flies busily.

**HABITAT** Ponds, lakes, ditches and brackish waters at up to 1,800m. Found across Europe from Ireland, and south from southern Scandinavia to North Africa.

**FOOD AND HABITS** Flies June–October. Feeds on insects. Usually seen in large numbers. Often perches on twigs.

# Common Blue Damselfly
*Enallagama cyathigerum*

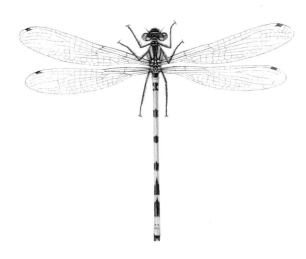

SIZE AND DESCRIPTION Length 29–36mm; hindwing 15–21mm. Male has a blue abdomen with black spots. Eighth and ninth segments are all-blue. Female has a yellowish or bluish abdomen, with variable dark markings. Strong flier.

HABITAT Pools, ponds, peat bogs and lakes. Found throughout Europe except Iceland and much of Mediterranean.

FOOD AND HABITS Flies mid-May–mid-September. May swarm in large numbers over water. Will pounce on dark spots on leaves, mistaking them for aphids.

# Brown Hawker
*Aeshna grandis*

**SIZE AND DESCRIPTION** Length 70–77mm; hindwing 41–49mm. Brown wings make this species unmistakable. Male has a brown abdomen with bright blue spots. Female has yellow markings on her brown abdomen. Both sexes have diagonal marks on the sides of the thorax. Strong flier.

**HABITAT** Ponds, lakes, canals, peat bogs and slow-flowing rivers. Absent from Iceland, Iberia, Italy, Greece, Scotland and northern Scandinavia.

**FOOD AND HABITS** Flies mid-June–mid-October. Hunts flies, mosquitoes, moths and butterflies.

# House Cricket
*Acheta domesticus*

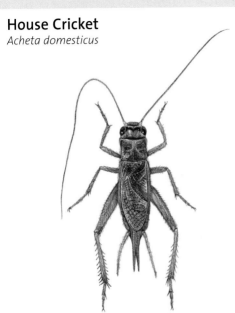

SIZE AND DESCRIPTION Length 16–20mm. Straw-coloured to brown body, with black marks on the head. Wings extend beyond the tip of the abdomen. Female has a straight ovipositor up to 15mm long.

HABITAT A native insect of Asia and Africa, but now widespread in Europe. Lives in buildings, but may also be found in refuse tips in summer. Song is a soft warble delivered at dusk or at night.

FOOD AND HABITS Feeds on refuse, but will also eat stored food.

# Common Field Grasshopper
*Chorthippus brunneus*

Length 14–18mm (m), 19–25mm (f). Colour grey, green, purple or black. Wings narrow, extending beyond the tip of the abdomen. Male's (and sometimes female's) abdomen has a reddish tip. Song a hard 'sst' sound, lasting about 0.2 seconds, repeated at 2-second intervals. Widespread in dry grassy habitats. Particularly common in southern England. Adults seen July–October.

# Oak Bush-cricket
*Meconema thalassinum*

Length 12–15mm. Pale green with wings extending beyond the tip of the abdomen. Female has a long, upwards-curving ovipositor. Male has two thin, inwards-curving cerci (paired appendages on rear-most segments), about 3mm long. Lives in trees, particularly oaks, and also found in gardens, in much of Europe, but not far north and far south. Adults seen July–October.

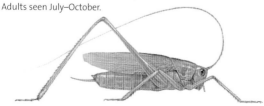

# Common Earwig
## *Forficula auricularia*

Length 10–15mm; pincers
4–9mm (m), 4–5mm (f).
Abundant in Europe in many
habitats; very common in
gardens. Mainly vegetarian.
Displays parental care. Female
lays 20–40 eggs in soil and cares
for them during winter. After they
hatch, she continues to feed and
tend the young even after they
come above ground.

# Common Cockroach
## *Blatta orientalis*

Length 18–30mm. Male's leathery
wings extend to the last three
segments of the abdomen. Female's
wings barely cover thorax. Found in
warm indoor places such as kitchens,
and rubbish tips in summer. Survives
outdoors in mild parts of Europe.
Originated in Asia and Africa.
Scavenges on the ground for food
scraps and decaying matter.

# Green Shield Bug
*Palomena prasina*

Length 10–15mm. Bright green in spring and summer, bronze-coloured in autumn. Wing-tips are dark brown. Inhabits woodland edges and glades, hedgerows, and gardens with shrubs and herbaceous borders across much of Europe. Eats the leaves of trees, shrubs and herbaceous plants. Hibernates in leaf litter.

# Common Flower Bug
*Anthocoris nemorum*

Length 3–4mm. Shiny and generally brownish, with a black spot on greyish forewings. Head is black. Found on almost any type of tree, shrub or herbaceous plant. Occurs across most of Europe. A predator of aphids, Red Spider Mites and other insects. Adults hibernate under loose bark and in clumps of grass.

# Common Backswimmer
*Notonecta glauca*

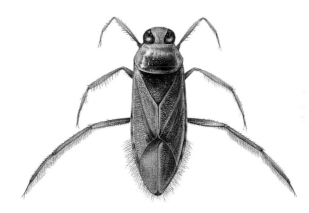

**SIZE AND DESCRIPTION** Length 16mm. Long and bristly hindlegs. Swims on its back, which is keeled, clutching a large air-bubble to its 'underside'. One of several water boatman species.

**HABITAT** Swims in still water, and will fly in warm weather. Widespread in Europe, including Britain.

**FOOD AND HABITS** Active all year round. A hunter of tadpoles, small fish and other insects.

# Common Pond Skater
*Gerris lacustris*

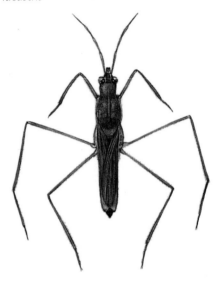

**SIZE AND DESCRIPTION** Length 10mm. Dark brown with a relatively narrow body and large eyes. Short forelegs, and long and slender hindlegs. Usually fully winged. There are several similar species.

**HABITAT** Lives on the surface of slow-moving water. In Britain not found in the Outer Hebrides or Shetland Isles.

**FOOD AND HABITS** Flies away from water to hibernate. When swimming it moves across the water's surface with a rowing action of the middle legs. The trailing hindlegs act as rudders, while the front legs catch insects that fall into the water.

# Woolly Aphid
*Eriosoma lanigerum*

Length 1–2mm. Purplish-brown with or without wings, and covered with strands of whitish fluffy wax. Inhabits orchards and gardens across Europe. Accidentally introduced from America. Sucks the sap of fruit trees. Most young are born live by parthogenesis (form of reproduction in which an unfertilized egg develops into a new individual, occurring quite commonly among insects).

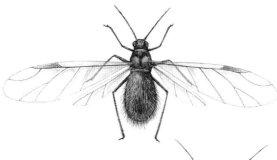

# Rose Aphid
*Macrosiphum rosae*

Length 1–2mm. Can be either green or pink. Long black cornicles on abdomen not found in other aphids. Occurs in woodland edges, hedges and gardens across Europe. Feeds on roses in spring, and scabious or teasel in summer.

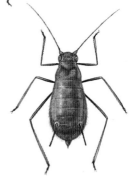

# Common Froghopper
## *Philaenus spumarius*

Length 6mm. Variable brown
pattern. Wings are held together
like a tent. Young coat themselves
in a white froth called 'cuckoo-
spit' – the sap of a plant that
has passed through them –
which acts as a protection from
predators and from drying out.
Adults do look a little like frogs
from above, and jump well. Found
on woody and herbaceous plants
throughout Europe except far
north. Flies June–September.
Feeds on plant sap.

# Potato Leafhopper
## *Eupteryx aurata*

Length 4mm. Black-and-yellow
pattern, often orange-tinged.
Wings reach past the tip of the
abdomen. Occurs on wasteland,
and in gardens and hedgerows
throughout Europe except far
north. Adults seen May–
December. Sucks sap from
herbaceous plants.

# Scorpion fly
## *Panorpa communis*

Length 15mm; wingspan
35mm. Head mounted
with large eyes, and
drawn into a prominent
upwards-pointing beak
opening at the tip of
the head. Scorpion-like
tip to male's abdomen
comprises complex
reproductive organs (it

is not a sting). Found in woods, hedgerows and shaded gardens in
Europe except far north. Flies May–August. Adults spend most of the
time crawling on vegetation in damp shady places near water and
along hedgerows. They scavenge mainly animal material.

# Green Lacewing
## *Chrysopa pallens*

Length 15–20mm;
wingspan 30–40mm.
Bright green body,
golden eyes and green
veins on transparent
wings. Several species
in continental Europe;
two similar species in

Britain. Inhabits woods, hedgerows, gardens and well-vegetated areas.
Found in most of Europe, but not Scotland and northern Scandinavia.
Flies May–August. Mainly nocturnal. Adults and larvae prey on aphids.

# Large White
## *Pieris brassicae*

Forewing 25–35mm. Black tips extend halfway down the forewing's edge. Upperside of the forewing has two black spots in female, one in male. Underside of the forewing has two spots

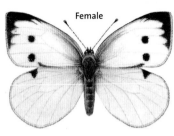

Female

in both sexes. Larva is green with black spots and yellow stripes. Lives in gardens and other flowery places. Flies April–October. Eggs are laid on the undersides of leaves. Larvae feed on brassicas and nasturtiums.

# Small White
## *Artogeia rapae*

Forewing 15–30mm. Upperside white with one black or grey spot on male's forewing and two on female's. Black or grey forewing patches extend further along the leading edge than down the side of the wing. Two spots on the underside of the forewing. Underside of the hindwing yellowish. Larva is green with a yellow stripe running along the sides. Abundant in gardens, hedges and flowery places in Europe. Flies March–October. Eggs are laid on leaves. Diet as Large White.

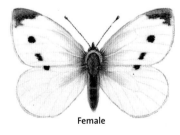

Female

# Brimstone
*Gonepteryx rhamni*

Forewing 25–30mm.
Male's wings sulphur-
yellow on top, paler
beneath. Female white
with a pale green tinge.
Larva is green with
white stripes along
the sides. Inhabits
open woodland,
gardens and flowery
places in Europe, but not most of Scotland and northern Scandinavia.
Flies February–September. Larvae eat Purging Buckthorn and Alder
Buckthorn. Adults overwinter in holly or ivy.

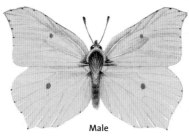

**Male**

# Orange Tip
*Anthocaris cardamines*

Forewing 20–25mm. Male has orange wing-tips and green blotches on
the underside of the hindwing. Female has greyish patches on the
forewing and mottled underwing. Lives in hedgerows, gardens, damp
meadows and woodland
margins. Found across
Europe except south-
west and southern
Spain, and far north. Flies
April–June. Larvae eat
Garlic Mustard and
Lady's Smock, and Sweet
Rocket and Honesty
in gardens.

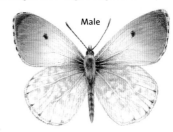

**Male**

# Holly Blue
*Celastrina argiolus*

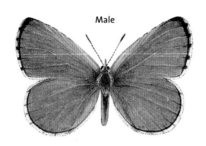

Male

**SIZE AND DESCRIPTION** Forewing 12–18mm. Upperside of male violet-blue. Female paler blue edged with a broad dark band, which is broader in the second brood. Undersides of the wings are pale blue-grey. Larva is small, green and slug-like. The blue most likely to be seen in gardens.

**HABITAT** Woodland margins, hedgerows, parks and gardens. Found throughout Europe except Scotland and northern Scandinavia.

**FOOD AND HABITS** Flies April–September. First brood feeds on flowers and the developing fruits of holly; second brood feeds on ivy. Adults drink honeydew, sap and the juices of carrion. Overwinters as a pupa.

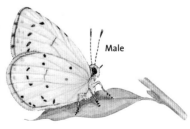

Male

# Small Tortoiseshell
*Aglais urticae*

Male

Male

**SIZE AND DESCRIPTION** Forewing 25mm. Upperside bright orange and black, with a row of blue spots on the edges of the wings. Larva is bristly and black.
**HABITAT** All kinds of flowery places. Common in Europe.
**FOOD AND HABITS** Flies March–October. Adults overwinter, often in buildings. Larvae feed on nettles, elms and hops.

# Peacock
*Inachis io*

**Male**

SIZE AND DESCRIPTION Forewing
30mm. Wings have four large
peacock-like 'eyes'. Upperside
orange, underside very dark
brown. Larva is black and bristly.
HABITAT Flowery places including
gardens. Occurs across Europe
to southern Scandinavia.
FOOD AND HABITS Flies March–May
and July–September. Larvae feed
on nettles. Adults often
overwinter in buildings.

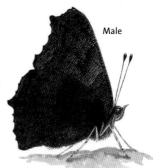

**Male**

# Comma
*Polygonia c-album*

Male

**SIZE AND DESCRIPTION** Forewing 23mm. Wings have jagged edges.
Upperside is orange with black and buff markings. Underside
of hindwing has a comma-shaped white mark. Larva is black
and sparsely bristled. Its rear end becomes white,
making it look like a bird dropping – a form of
protection from predators.

Male

**HABITAT** Woodland margins, gardens, hedges
and other flowery places. Common across
Europe, but absent from Ireland,
northern Britain and far north.

**FOOD AND HABITS** Flies March–
September, in two broods. Second
brood is darker than first. Adults
overwinter, hanging from leaves.
Larvae feed on nettles, hops and elms.

# Painted Lady
*Cynthia cardui*

Male

**SIZE AND DESCRIPTION** Forewing 20–25mm. Upperside orange with a black forewing tip patched with white. Underside pale with three blue underwing spots. Black larva has tufts of hairs and a yellow-and-red stripe down each side.

**HABITAT** Flowery places including roadsides and gardens. Occurs throughout Europe, but is a migrant from North Africa. Does not survive European winters.

Male

**FOOD AND HABITS** Flies April–November, arriving in Britain in late spring to early summer. Produces only two broods in Europe, and throughout the year in North Africa. Feeds on thistles and sometimes nettles.

# Red Admiral
*Vanessa atalanta*

Male

**SIZE AND DESCRIPTION** Forewing 30mm. Upperside velvety dark brown with bright orange bars on each wing. Tips of the forewings are black with white markings. Underside of the hindwing is pale brown, while underside of forewing shows orange, blue and white markings. Dark larva has bristles and a pale yellow stripe along each side.

Male

**HABITAT** Flowery places across Europe except northern Scandinavia. Resident in southern Europe, moving north in spring.

**FOOD AND HABITS** Flies May–October, in two broods. Larvae feed on nettles. Adults feed on rotting fruits in autumn.

# Gatekeeper
*Pyronia tithonus*

**Male**

**SIZE AND DESCRIPTION** Forewing 17–25mm. Orange patches on the wings. Black 'eyes' with two highlights at the tops of the forewings. Green or brown larva.

**HABITAT** Hedgerows, woodland margins and gardens. Found in southern Britain and Ireland, and south across the rest of Europe.

**FOOD AND HABITS** Flies July–September. Larval foodplants are fine-leaved grasses. Adults are fond of Bramble blossom and Marjoram.

**Male**

# Lackey Moth
## *Malacosoma neustria*

Forewing 13–20mm. Occurs in a range of browns. Darker wing bands curve inwards. Long and tufted grey-blue larva has white, orange, black and yellow stripes along the body. Found in many habitats across Europe, but not

Scotland and northern Scandinavia. Flies June–August at night. Single-brooded. Larvae live in colonies in cocoons, feeding on the leaves of Blackthorn, hawthorn, plums and sallows. Overwinters as an egg.

# Winter Moth
## *Operophtera brumata*

Forewing 15mm. Males have greyish-brown wings with a faint pattern; females have stunted relict wings. Green looper larva is about 20mm long. Abundant wherever there are trees and shrubs. Flies October–February. Nocturnal and attracted to lighted windows. Females can be seen on windowsills and tree trunks. Larvae feed on deciduous trees. Favours hard fruits, especially apples.

# Peppered Moth
## *Biston betularia*

Forewing 20–30mm.
Variable. Normal form
white, peppered with
fine dark marks, or sooty
black. Green or brown
looper larva is up to
60mm long. Found in
woods, gardens, scrub
and parks across Europe
except far north. Flies
May–August, coming to lighted windows. Larvae feed on a range
of trees and shrubs, including sallows, hawthorn, Golden Rod
and Raspberry.

# Peach Blossom
## *Thyatira batis*

Forewing 15mm. Forewings are brown with pink blotches. Larva is dark
brown with slanting white lines and bumps on its back. Found in
woodland and woodland edges in northern and central Europe,
including Britain. Flies
May–August at night.
One brood a year.
Larvae feed on Bramble,
Raspberry and
Blackberry. Overwinters
as a pupa.

# Magpie Moth
*Abraxas grossulariata*

**SIZE AND DESCRIPTION** Forewing 20mm. Variable black-and-white pattern with a yellowish-orange line across the middle of the forewing and near the head. Looper larva is about 30mm long, and pale green with black spots and a rusty line along each side.

**HABITAT** Woods, gardens and hedgerows.

**FOOD AND HABITS** Flies June–August. Larvae feed on Blackthorn, hawthorn and many other shrubs. Overwinters as a small larva and pupates in May–June.

Caterpillar

# Privet Hawkmoth
## *Sphinx ligustri*

Forewing 41–55mm.
Brown wings have black
markings, and there is a
tan trailing edge to the
forewing. Body striped
with pink and black.
Body is up to 100mm
long, and green with

purple-and-white stripes on each side of its body. Occurs in woodland
edges, hedges, parks and gardens across Europe except Ireland,
Scotland and far north. Flies June–July, drinking nectar on the wing,
especially from honeysuckle. Larvae feed on privets, Ash and Lilac.

# White Ermine
## *Spilosoma lubricipeda*

Forewing 17mm. White
with more or less sparse
black spots. Hairy thorax
and black-spotted yellow
abdomen. Larva is up to
45mm long, dark brown
and very hairy, with a
dark red line down its

back. Found in hedgerows, gardens, waste ground and other habitats
throughout Europe. Flies May–August, in 1–2 broods. Adults do not
feed, but larvae feed on herbaceous plants, including docks and
numerous garden plants.

# Garden Tiger
*Arctia caja*

**SIZE AND DESCRIPTION** Forewing 25–35mm. Chocolate-brown forewings have cream patterning. Hindwings are orange with black spots. Very hairy black-and-brown larva is known as a 'woolly bear'.
**HABITAT** Open habitats, including gardens and scrub, across Europe.
**FOOD AND HABITS** Flies June–August. Larvae feed on herbaceous plants. Winters as a small larva.

Caterpillar

# Setaceous Hebrew Character
*Xestia c-nigrum*

Forewing to 20mm.
Greyish-brown to
chestnut with a purplish
tinge. There is a pale
patch on the leading
edge of the forewing.
The larva is initially
green, before becoming
pale greenish-grey.

Found in lowland areas including cultivated regions, woodland
and marshes throughout Europe except far north. Flies May–
October. Two or more broods a year. Larvae feed on a wide range
of herbaceous plants.

# Green Arches
*Anaplectoides prasina*

Forewing 20mm.
Greenish forewings
have variable black
markings, while
hindwings are dark
grey or brown. Larva
is brown with darker
markings. Inhabits

deciduous woodland over most of Europe. Flies mid-June–mid-July
at night. Larvae feed on a range of plants, especially honeysuckle
and Bilberry.

# Grey Dagger
## *Acronicta psi*

Forewing to 20mm.
Pale to dark grey,
with dark, apparently
dagger-shaped marks.
Hairy grey-black larva
has a yellow line along
its back, red spots
along its sides and a

black horn on its first abdominal segment. Occurs in woodland,
commons, parks and gardens across Europe except far north. Flies
May–September, with larva feeding August–October on a wide
range of broadleaved trees.

# Angle Shades
## *Phlogophora meticulosa*

Forewing 25mm. Varies
from brown to green,
with distinctive V-
shaped markings.
Forewing's trailing
edge has a ragged look,
exaggerated by its
habit of resting with
its wings curled over.

Fat green larva is up to 45mm long and has a white line (often faint)
along its back. A migrant found in almost any habitat in Europe. Flies
most of the year, but mainly May–October. Larvae feed on a variety of
wild and cultivated plants. Overwinters as a larva.

# Large Yellow Underwing
*Noctua pronuba*

**SIZE AND DESCRIPTION** Forewing 25mm. Varies from pale to dark brown. Hindwings are deep yellow with a black border. The yellow flashes when the moth takes flight, which is thought to confuse predators. Green larva is up to 50mm long with two rows of dark markings on its back.

**HABITAT** Well-vegetated habitats throughout Europe except far north.

**FOOD AND HABITS** Flies June–October. Flight is fast and erratic. The yellow flashes shown in flight become invisible the moment it lands.

# Red Underwing
*Catocala nupta*

**SIZE AND DESCRIPTION** Forewing 30–35mm. Grey-mottled forewings make this moth well camouflaged on tree bark, but bright red underwings are very conspicuous in flight. Pale brown larva has warty bud-like lumps on its back.

**HABITAT** Woodlands, hedges, gardens and parks throughout Europe except northern Scandinavia.

**FOOD AND HABITS** Flies August–September at night. Flies erratically, flashing its red underwings to confuse predators. Larvae feed in May–July on willows, poplars and aspens.

# Common Crane-fly
*Tipula paludosa*

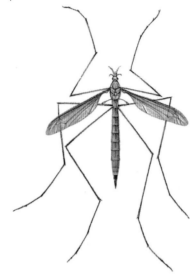

**Size and description** Length 25mm. Dark brown along the leading edges of the wings. Female's wings are shorter than her abdomen. Male has a square-ended abdomen, while female's is pointed, with an ovipositor. Dull brown grub is known as a 'leather-jacket'. Also called Daddy-long-legs.

**Habitat** Common in grasslands, parks and gardens throughout Europe.

**Food and habits** Flies throughout the year, but most numerous in autumn. Adults rarely feed. Grubs live in the soil and appear at night to gnaw the bases of plant stems.

# Large Bee-fly
*Bombylius major*

Length 10–12mm; wingspan
20–25mm. Brown, furry and bee-
like coat, and a long proboscis.
Dark leading edges to the wings.
Legs are long and slender.
Inhabits sunny wooded places
across Europe, but rare in far
north. Hovers, using its long front
legs to steady itself as it reaches
for nectar with its long proboscis.
Female drops eggs in flight, and
larvae develop as parasites in
solitary bee and wasps' nests.

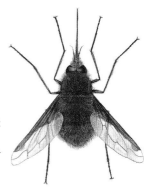

# Cleg-fly
*Haematopota pluvialis*

Length 11mm. Dull grey horsefly
with a rather cylindrical
abdomen. Wings are mottled,
and held above abdomen when
at rest. Flies silently. Common
in May–September, especially
in damp woods. Replaced in
northern and upland areas by

another similar species. Flies May–October. Most active in humid
and overcast weather. Females are bloodsuckers, biting humans
and livestock. Males drink nectar and plant juices. Larvae live in
damp soil, where they prey on other invertebrates.

# Syrphus-fly
## *Syrphus ribesii*

Length 10mm. Yellow-and-
black-striped with a rounded
abdomen. Larva is green and
slug-like. There are several similar
species. Found in flower-rich
habitats across Europe. Flying
adults seen March–November.
Males perch on leaves or twigs
up to 2.5m from the ground and
make a high-pitched whining
noise. Feeds mainly on nectar,
but will also crush and swallow
pollen. Larvae feed on aphids
and are themselves victims
of parasitic wasps.

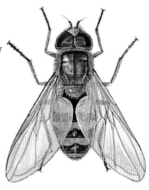

# Narcissus-fly
## *Merodon equestris*

Length 10–15mm. A bumblebee
mimic. Occurs in gardens, parks,
woods and hedges throughout
Europe. Flies March–August.
Larvae burrow down
into bulbs.

# Bluebottle
*Calliphora vomitoria*

Length 12–15mm. Rounded
metallic-blue body. Carrot-
shaped creamy white larva.
Widespread throughout
Europe. Often flies in and
around houses. Can be seen
all year round, often sunning
itself on walls. Females lay
eggs on meat and carrion, on
which the larvae feed. Males
can often be seen on flowers,
feeding on the nectar.

# Greenbottle
*Lucilia caesar*

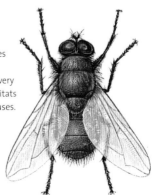

Length 8–15mm. Abdomen varies
from blue-green to emerald,
becoming coppery with age. Silvery
below eyes. Occurs in most habitats
in Europe. Common around houses.
Active all year round. Feeds on
nectar, carrion and wounds.

# Common Carrot-fly
*Psila rosae*

Length 4mm. Black thorax
and abdomen with brown
legs. Creamy white grub.
Found in gardens and on
farmland. Lays eggs in late
spring near young carrots.
Larvae infest the roots,
often turning them into
empty shells.

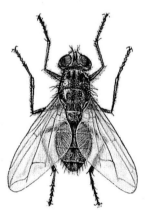

# Common House-fly
*Musca domestica*

Length 8mm. Black and tan
abdomen. Found in and around
houses throughout Europe.
Especially numerous in places
where there is plenty of decaying
matter. Occurs during most of
the year, but is most common
June–September.

# Celery Fly
## *Euleia heraclei*

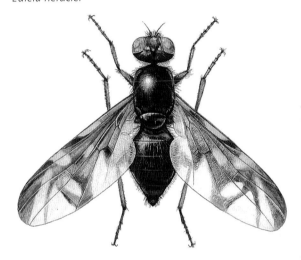

**SIZE AND DESCRIPTION** Length 6mm. Wings mottled dark or reddish-brown. Body bulbous.

**HABITAT** Found in gardens and open countryside where umbellifers grow, in most of Europe.

**FOOD AND HABITS** Flies April–November. Larvae eat the leaves of umbellifers from the insides, causing brownish mines.

# Yellow Ophion
*Ophion luteus*

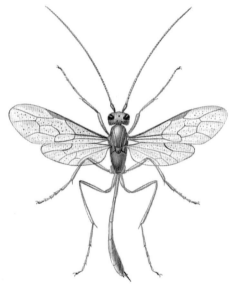

**SIZE AND DESCRIPTION** Length 15–20mm. Yellowish-brown with a strongly arched abdomen and thorax. Large black eyes.

**HABITAT** Well-vegetated habitats in most of Europe except far north.

**FOOD AND HABITS** Adults fly July–October. Attracted by lighted windows. Feeds on nectar and pollen. Eggs are laid in larvae or pupae of several species. Usually one grub per host. Adult always emerges from the host's pupa.

# Horntail
*Urceros gigas*

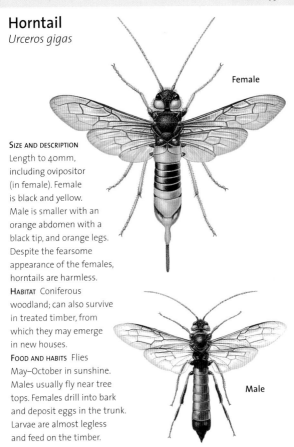

Female

**SIZE AND DESCRIPTION**
Length to 40mm,
including ovipositor
(in female). Female
is black and yellow.
Male is smaller with an
orange abdomen with a
black tip, and orange legs.
Despite the fearsome
appearance of the females,
horntails are harmless.
**HABITAT** Coniferous
woodland; can also survive
in treated timber, from
which they may emerge
in new houses.
**FOOD AND HABITS** Flies
May–October in sunshine.
Males usually fly near tree
tops. Females drill into bark
and deposit eggs in the trunk.
Larvae are almost legless
and feed on the timber.

Male

# Red Ant
## *Myrmica rubra*

Length 4–5mm (worker).
Workers chestnut-brown. Males
and queens, which appear in
late summer and early autumn,
about one-and-a-half times
as long as workers. Males
have longer and less bulbous
abdomens than females. Red
Ants can sting. Occurs in
open habitats across Europe.
Omnivorous, tending towards
animal food.

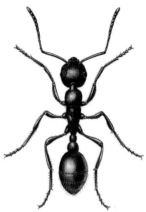

# Black Garden Ant
## *Lasius niger*

Length to 5mm (worker).
Workers black or dark brown.
Flying ants, which emerge
July–August, are males and
females. They are about twice
the size of workers. Black
Garden Ants do not sting.
Occurs in open habitats across
Europe, including gardens.
Omnivorous, but especially
fond of sweet foods – will 'milk'
aphids for their honeydew.

# Common Wasp
## *Vespula vulgaris*

**Size and description** Length 11–14mm (worker). Black and yellow with four yellow spots at the rear of the thorax. Yellow marks on either side of the thorax usually have parallel sides.

**Habitat** Common in most habitats across Europe.

**Food and habits** Usually nests in well-drained underground sites such as hedge banks, but also uses cavities in walls and lofts. Nests are built of yellowish paper.

▶ **Similar species German Wasp** (*V. germanica*). 12–16mm long (worker). Like Common Wasp, but with marks on either side of the thorax bulge. Common in most habitats except far north. Nesting similar to Common Wasp, but nest paper is greyer and less brittle.

# Hornet
*Vespa crabro*

**SIZE AND DESCRIPTION** Length 18–25mm (worker). Chestnut-brown and yellow in colour.
**HABITAT** Wooded areas, parks and gardens throughout most of Europe, but not Scotland, Ireland and northern Scandinavia.
**FOOD AND HABITS** Nests in hollow trees, wall cavities and chimneys. Preys on insects as large as butterflies and dragonflies to feed young.

# Honey Bee
*Apis mellifera*

Size and description
Length 12–15mm.
Queens are about
20mm long, but are
rarely seen outside the
nest. Colours vary. Can
be identified by a
narrow cell near the tip
of the wing's leading edge. Male has a stouter body than female.

Habitat Found almost everywhere in Europe, but becoming
increasingly scarce.

Food and habits Flies spring–late autumn. Lives in colonies with
a single queen. Males, or drones, appear spring–summer in small
numbers. Nests contain combs of hexagonal cells, used for rearing
grubs and storing pollen and honey.

▶ Similar species **Tawny Mining Bee** (*Andrena fulva*). 10–12mm long.
Female has a bright yellow abdomen; male is smaller and dark.
Favours open habitats
including gardens, parks
and woodland edges, in
central and southern
Europe, including
southern England. Flies
April–June. Nests in the
ground, especially on
lawns, throwing spoil
from nest hole into a
small volcano-like
mound. Solitary species.

# Buff-tailed Bumblebee
## *Bombus terrestris*

SIZE AND DESCRIPTION
Length 20–22mm.
Orange collar and
second abdominal
segment. Tip of the
abdomen is buffish-
white; queen's abdominal
tip is buffish in Britain,
but white elsewhere.

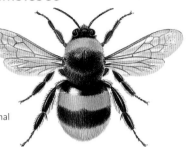

HABITAT Well-vegetated habitats across Europe.

FOOD AND HABITS Queens visit sallow catkins in March–April; workers visit apple and cherry blossoms. Nests well below ground level.

▼ SIMILAR SPECIES **White-tailed Bumblebee** (*B. lucorum*). 20–22mm long. Yellow collar and second abdominal segment, with a white tip to the abdomen. Inhabits well-vegetated places across Europe. A very early flier, with queens emerging in February and feeding on sallow catkins. Nests below ground.

# Garden Bumblebee
*Bombus hortorum*

**SIZE AND DESCRIPTION** Length 20–24mm. Collar, rear of the thorax and first segment of the abdomen are yellow. Tip of the abdomen is whitish. Fairly 'scruffy' appearance, with long hair. Tongue is as long as the body.

**HABITAT** Common in well-vegetated habitats, especially in gardens, throughout Europe.

**FOOD AND HABITS** Queens often seen on White Dead-nettle. Exceptionally long tongue allows it to obtain nectar from plants with deep-tubed flowers. Nests on or just beneath the ground, typically in banks and among tree roots. Like many other bumblebee species, has undergone a decline due mainly to changes in agricultural practices that have lead to loss of habitats and foodplants.

# Devil's Coach Horse
*Staphylinus olens*

Length 20–30mm. Long-bodied black rove beetle with small and almost square elytra (wing-cases), which leave the long abdomen exposed. Inhabits woods, hedges, parks and gardens throughout Europe. Often found in damp outhouses. Nocturnal predator with powerful jaws. Feeds on slugs, worms, woodlice and other invertebrates. When under threat it raises its tail and opens its jaws.

# Cockchafer
*Melolontha melolontha*

Length 20–30mm. Black thorax. Rusty elytra do not quite cover the abdomen, exposing the pointed tip. Legs are brown and the antennae fan out. Male has larger antennae than female. Whitish larva has a brown head. Inhabits woodland margins, parks and gardens throughout Europe, but absent above 1,000m and from far north. Flies May–July at night. Adults chew the leaves of trees and shrubs. Larvae, which take three years to develop, feed on roots.

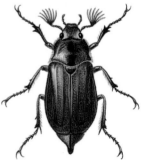

# Rose Chafer
## *Cetonia aurata*

Length 14–18mm. Flattened
squarish elytra are green, but
may be bronze or bluish-black.
Found in woodland margins,
hedges, scrub and gardens in
southern and central Europe,
including southern England. Adults
fly May–August by day, and nibble
the petals and stamens of flowers.
Larvae feed in decaying wood,
taking 2–3 years to develop.

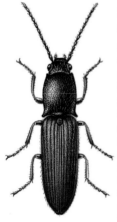

# Click Beetle
## *Athous haemorrhoidalis*

Length 7–10mm. Long black or dark
brown thorax and ridged brown back.
Larva is brown with a thin segmented
body. Found in grassland, including
parks and gardens, across Europe except
far north. Flies May–July. Adults chew
grasses and flowers, especially stamens
with pollen. Larvae, called 'wireworms',
cause severe damage to roots. Click
beetles are so-called because if they
find themselves on their back, they can
snap their thoracic segments with an
audible 'click', causing their body to flip
in the air to right themselves .

# Carabid Beetle
*Carabus nemoralis*

Length 20–30mm. Black tinged with
metallic colours varying from bronze
to brassy green. Elytra are pitted in
lines and finely ridged. Female is less
shiny than male. Occurs in most
habitats throughout Europe, but
not northern Scandinavia. Fast-
moving flightless beetle that is
a nocturnal predator of ground-
dwelling invertebrates.

# Violet Ground Beetle
*Carabus violaceus*

Length 20–35mm. Black with violet
tinges to the thorax and elytra.
Thorax is flanged and the elytra
have a smooth oval shape. Larva has
a shiny black head and thorax, and a
long, segmented dusky body. Found
in woods, hedges, gardens and scrub.
Non-flying, fast-running nocturnal
predator of invertebrates. Larva is
also a predator, but is less agile than
the adult beetle.

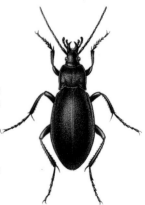

# Cardinal Beetle
*Pyrochroa coccinea*

Length 14–18mm. Bright reddish-orange elytra and thorax, with a black head and feathery antennae. Black legs. Larvae are yellowish-brown with a squarish rear end. Found in woodland edges in northern and central Europe. Flies May–July. Found on flowers and old tree trunks. Larvae live under bark and prey on other insects.

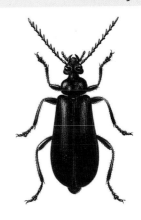

# Soldier Beetle
*Cantharis rustica*

Length 11–14mm. Black elytra. Orange thorax bears a dark mark. Beaded antennae. Larva has a flattened and segmented dark brown body with a pair of legs on each of the first three segments. Abundant throughout Europe in damp situations, including woodland edges and open country. Flies May–August. Preys on other insects, which it finds on flower blossoms.

# Pea Weevil
## *Sitona lineatus*

Length 4–5mm. Pale and dark brown stripes run along the body. Eyes are very prominent. Found wherever wild and cultivated leguminous plants grow. Native to Europe, but absent from far north. Adults, which are mainly active in spring and autumn, chew semi-circular pieces from the edges of leaves and may damage seedlings. Larvae live inside root nodules. There are several species of weevil that attack garden plants.

# Potato Flea Beetle
## *Psylliodes affinis*

Length 2.8mm. Reddish-brown beetle with thick black thighs on its hind legs. Common on nightshades and potatoes in Europe, including southern and central Britain. Adults nibble leaves, while larvae feed on roots. Beetles hibernate under bark and leaf litter, emerging in spring to resume feeding.

# Stag Beetle
## *Lucanus cervus*

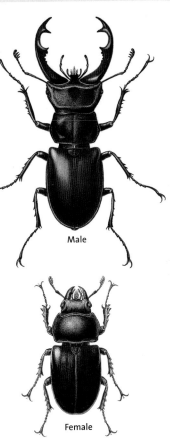

SIZE AND DESCRIPTION Length 25–75mm. Smooth dark-tan elytra, and black head and thorax. Male's huge jaws look like antlers (hence the name). Whitish larva has a brown head.

HABITAT Oakwoods, parks and gardens in England, and in central and southern Europe. In Britain, may be seen in gardens in London and elsewhere in the south-east. Becoming rare everywhere.

FOOD AND HABITS Flies May–August in the evenings and at night. Feeds on tree sap. 'Antlers' are used by breeding males for grappling with each other – males are harmless to humans. Larvae take about three years to mature. They feed on rotting wood.

Male

Female

# Seven-spot Ladybird
*Coccinella 7-punctata*

SIZE AND DESCRIPTION
Length 5.2–8mm.
Bright-red elytra
with seven black
spots. Larva is steely
blue with yellow or
cream spots.
HABITAT Abundant
in well-vegetated
habitats in Europe.
FOOD AND HABITS Flies
early spring–autumn.
Adults and larvae feed
on aphids. Passes
winter in small groups or individually in leaf
litter and sheltered places near the ground.

▼ SIMILAR SPECIES **Twenty-two-
spot Ladybird** (*Thea 22-
punctata*). 5mm long. Lemon
yellow with 10–11 black spots
on each elytron and five spots
on the pronotum. Inhabits
well-vegetated places across
Europe. Flies April–August.
Eats mildew on umbellifers
and other plants. Winters in
leaf litter, but may appear in
mild weather.

# European Long-tailed Scorpion
*Euscorpius flavicaudis*

**SIZE AND DESCRIPTION** Length 35–45mm. Dark brown body and pincers, and paler legs. Sting on the end of its tail is yellowish.

**HABITAT** An uncommon species found in southern and central Europe, including in gardens; favours cracks in old walls. In Britain there is a well-known colony at the docks in Sheerness in Kent, where it arrived by boat in the 1860s; small colonies are reputed to exist elsewhere.

**FOOD AND HABITS** Most active at night, taking cover during the day. Feeds on small insects, spiders, woodlice and other scorpions. Ambushes prey from the entrance to its home, and despatches it with its claws. Mildly venomous and rarely uses its sting, which is like a bee sting to humans.

# Garden Spider
*Araneus diadematus*

SIZE AND DESCRIPTION  Length to 18mm (f), 9mm (m). Abdomen bears
a white cross. Colours vary from pale yellowish-brown to very
dark brown. Male has a smaller abdomen than female. Also called
Cross Spider.

HABITAT  Common in woodland, heathland, gardens and hedges across
northern Europe.

FOOD AND HABITS  A web-spinner that preys on flies and other insects.
In autumn the female lays up to 800 eggs in a single mass; they are
protected by a layer of silk. She stays with them until her death a
month later. The classic orb webs of these spiders are most obvious
in late summer–autumn, when the spiders mature.

**How an orb web is made**

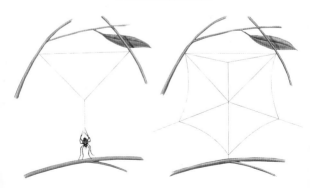

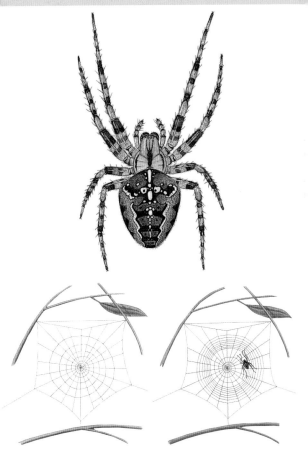

# Green Orb-weaver
## *Araniella cucurbitina*

Length 3.5–6mm. Female has a green abdomen with dark brown spots, and a brown head and legs. Slightly smaller male has a smaller abdomen and an orange-brown head. Found in low bushes and trees across Europe. Adults are seen summer–autumn. Web is small and haphazard. Egg sacs are attached to the undersides of leaves and covered by a mass of silk. The leaves bearing the egg sacs fall to the ground; young emerge in spring.

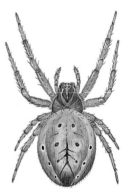

# Common Orb-weaver
## *Meta segmentata*

Length 4–8mm. Colours are very variable, but the pattern on the abdomen is more or less constant. Abundant in gardens and other well-vegetated habits that will support its orb web. Adults mature late summer–autumn. When disturbed, male especially stretches his legs forwards along leaves or stems. Web is slung from vegetation up to 2m above ground. Spherical egg sacs are attached to vegetation near the nest.

# Missing Sector Orb-weaver
*Zygiella x-notata*

SIZE AND DESCRIPTION Length to 9mm (f), 6mm (m). Leaf-like dark pattern fringed with pink on the abdomen. Very long front legs. Male is similar to female, but smaller.

HABITAT Widespread throughout Europe except Finland. Favours human habitation.

FOOD AND HABITS Slings a vertical web around window- and door-frames. There are empty sectors at the top of the web, hence the common name of this spider. Waits in a crevice for insect prey to become trapped in the web.

# Wasp Spider
*Argiope bruennichi*

**SIZE AND DESCRIPTION**
Length to 25mm (f),
7mm (m). Female is
much larger and more
colourful than male,
with a black-and-
yellow-barred abdomen.
**HABITAT** Near field
edges, in woodland
clearings, on waste
ground and in gardens. Found in Europe as far as Sweden. In Britain it
was first discovered in Sussex in the 1940s.
**FOOD AND HABITS** Adults seen June–September. Low-built orb-type web
traps jumping insects such as grasshoppers. Female lays eggs in a
large and fluffy egg sac close to the web. This has thick zigzag
stitching (stabilimentum) worked into the centre (purpose disputed).

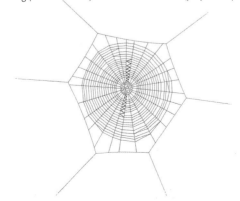

# Giant House Spider
*Tegenaria duellica*

**SIZE AND DESCRIPTION** Length to 16mm
(f), 14mm (m). A grey-brown sheet-
web weaver with pale markings.
Male is smaller than female, but has
longer (50–60mm) legs. Among
the largest of European spiders.
**HABITAT** Widespread in northern
Europe near human habitation
and in rocky and wooded places.
**FOOD AND HABITS** May be seen
running across floors at night,
especially in the autumn, when the
males are seeking mates. Builds
a triangular web with a tubular
retreat in the corner, where it waits
for its prey to become entrapped.
Females may live for many years.

# Mothercare Spider
*Theridion sisyphium*

**Size and description** Length 2.5–4mm. Brown thorax and a boldly marked abdomen. Female is slightly larger than male.

**Habitat** Widespread in northern Europe in woodland margins, scrub, hedges and gardens.

**Food and habits** Female spins a three-dimensional web of criss-cross strands on bushes, particularly gorse, making a retreat at the top, where she rears her brood. She guards her greenish-blue egg sac and feeds her young by regurgitation. Maturity is reached in summer.

# Rabbit Hutch Spider
*Steatodea bipunctata*

**SIZE AND DESCRIPTION** Length to 8mm (f), 5mm (m). Female has a reddish-brown abdomen with thin pale markings near the thorax. Male has a narrow white marking down the centre of the abdomen and much larger palps (which contain sex organs).

**HABITAT** Widespread around houses and outbuildings in northern Europe. Sometimes found in rabbit hutches, hence its name.

**FOOD AND HABITS** Females found all year, males only in summer–autumn. Males have ridges and teeth under the carapace and abdomen, with which they create sounds to attract females.

# Toothed Weaver
*Textrix denticulata*

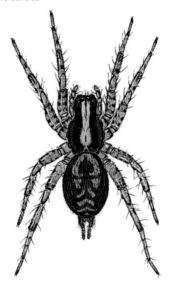

**Size and description** Length 6–7mm. Male and female are similar in size and appearance. Spinnerets (glands that spin silk threads), located at the base of the abdomen, are especially prominent.
**Habitat** Widespread throughout northern Europe, both in open countryside and homes.
**Food and habits** Females are seen throughout the year, males in summer only. Often seen running over warm ground in summer. Web is a triangular sheet with a tunnel-like retreat at the apex.

# Red-and-white Cobweb Weaver
*Enoplognatha ovata*

**Size and description** Length 3–6mm. Very pale brown thorax. Abdomen is creamy with two pink bands (as shown), a single broad pink band or no band, but always with pairs of black dots. Male is smaller than female and has a smaller abdomen. Also called Candy-stripe Spider.
**Habitat** Low vegetation and bushes.
**Food and habits** Flimsy three-dimensional web has sticky outer sections for trapping small insects. Female guards her bluish egg sac beneath a leaf, which is often rolled. Maturity is reached in summer.

# Hammock Sheet-weaver
*Linyphia triangularis*

**SIZE AND DESCRIPTION** Length
5–6.6mm. Female's abdomen
is roughly triangular in profile,
and pale in colour with brown
triangular marks down the
centre. Male's abdomen is
slimmer and lacks any
triangular marks.
**HABITAT** Widespread in Europe
wherever there are trees or
other plants with stiff foliage.
**FOOD AND HABITS** Adults seen
midsummer–late autumn.
Slings a hammock-like web in
bushes, then hangs beneath
the web and waits for insects
to fall into it.

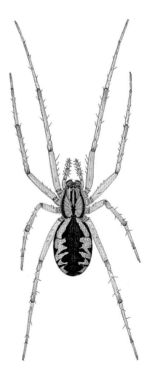

# Lace Weaver Spider
*Amaurobius similis*

SIZE AND DESCRIPTION Length
9–12mm (f), 6–8mm (m).
Colour of abdomen varies
from green to brown, and
contains dark marks.
HABITAT Common and
widespread near human
habitation across Europe.
FOOD AND HABITS Female found
throughout most of the year,
but male seen only in late
summer–autumn. Spins a
lace-like web across a small
hole or crevice in which it
hides. Web can have a scruffy
and patchy appearance.

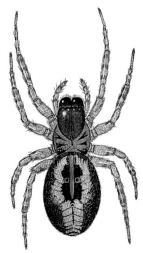

# Downy Jumper
*Sitticus pubescens*

**Size and description** Length 4–5mm. Dull brown in colour, but with light patches and covered with light hairs. Sexes are similar, but male has a smaller abdomen than female. Like Zebra Spider (opposite) and other jumping spiders, has two very large forwards-facing eyes; the six other eyes are smaller.

**Habitat** Usually near human habitation. Widespread but localized across northern Europe.

**Food and habits** Hunts prey by stalking and leaping upon it. Jumps well. Its very good eyesight enables it to work out how far to jump to reach its prey. Jumping spiders rarely spin webs.

# Zebra Spider
*Salticus scenicus*

SIZE AND DESCRIPTION
Length 5–7mm. Hairy, and black with variable white marks (hence the common name). Legs are greyish. Short front legs and extremely large eyes. Male is smaller than female.

HABITAT Widespread throughout northern Europe. Often found on walls and fences near human habitation.

FOOD AND HABITS Adults evident May–August. Stalks prey using its keen eyesight, which enables it to detect movement as much as 30cm away, then leaps upon it. Active in warm weather, especially in sunshine.

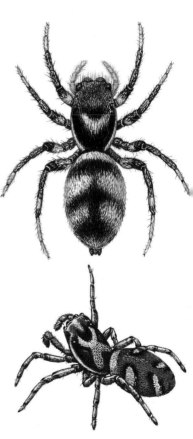

# Fillet Sac Spider
## *Clubiona comta*

Length 3–6mm. Pale brown thorax and legs. Brown abdomen with creamy markings. Male is slightly smaller than female. Common in northern Europe in any habitat with trees and bushes. Found spring–summer. Nocturnal hunter that spends the daytime hidden in silken cells under stones, among vegetation or under bark.

# Spotted Wolf Spider
## *Pardosa amentata*

Length 5.5–8mm. Dark and variably patterned. Male is smaller than female. Widespread in northern Europe in low-growing vegetation and on open ground. Female seen spring–autumn; male disappears after midsummer. Female carries eggs in a silken sac attached to her spinnerets. When the young spiders hatch, they climb onto her back and are carried for a short time.

**Female with egg sac**

# Nursery-web Spider
*Pisaura mirabilis*

SIZE AND DESCRIPTION Length 10–15mm. Sexes are similar, but male is smaller than female and has a narrower abdomen. Colours vary from yellow to brown, with markings that may be very clear or even absent.

HABITAT Widespread in grassland, heathland, woodland and gardens across northern Europe.

FOOD AND HABITS Seen in summer. Diurnal hunter. Runs swiftly and suns itself on plants. Female carries her egg-cocoon with her fangs. She later spins a silken tent over it, then stands guard until the young disperse.

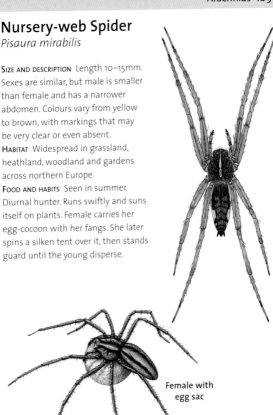

Female with egg sac

# Water Spider
*Argyroneta aquatica*

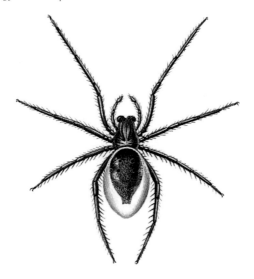

**SIZE AND DESCRIPTION** Length to 15mm. Brown and rather mouse-like.
**HABITAT** Ponds, lakes, dykes and sluggish streams across Europe.
**FOOD AND HABITS** Builds a diving bell by trapping air in the middle of a
sheet-like web spun among pond plants underwater. Visits the surface
and collects air between the hairs on its abdomen, releasing this into
the diving bell by stroking the hairs on its back legs. Lives in the bell,
leaving it only to hunt for food such as small fish, tadpoles and other
pond life. May spend winter sealed inside an old snail's shell.

# Woodlouse Spider
*Dysdera crocata*

**Size and description** Length to 15mm (f), 10mm (m). Fleshy-brown thorax and legs. Abdomen whitish. Male is slightly smaller than female, and has a narrower abdomen.

**Habitat** Found under stones, logs and other material in gardens and slightly damp habitats. Widespread in Europe except Scandinavia.

**Food and habits** Found all year round. Feeds on woodlice, which it catches and crushes with its fangs. Nocturnal, spending the day under cover in a silken cell, in which its eggs are laid.

# Leopard Spider
*Segestria senoculata*

**SIZE AND DESCRIPTION** Length 7–10mm. Black head, and pale legs and abdomen. Male resembles female, but has a smaller abdomen.
**HABITAT** Lives in holes in walls and bark throughout Europe.
**FOOD AND HABITS** Adults seen spring–autumn. Hides within holes from which about a dozen silky trip-wires spread out. When prey disturbs the threads, it dashes out of its hole to grab it.

# Flower Spider
*Misumena vatia*

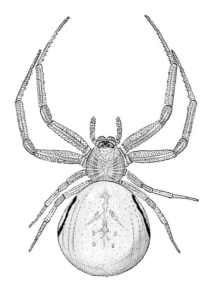

Size and description Length to 10mm (f), 5mm (m). Female is white, yellow or greenish with reddish stripes on each side of her abdomen (although these may be absent). Male has dark brown stripes on his abdomen, and two dark brown front pairs of legs.

Habitat Flowery areas. Widespread in northern Europe, but more common in southern part of its range.

Food and habits Seen in summer. Sits in white and yellow flowers waiting in ambush for prey. Crab spiders do not spin webs.

# Common Crab Spider
*Xysticus cristatus*

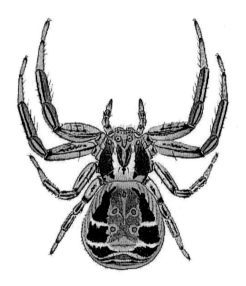

**SIZE AND DESCRIPTION** Length 3–8mm. Abdomen has triangular markings; patterns are variable. Female may be almost twice the size of male. Like other crab spiders, it moves with a rather crab-like sideways gait.

**HABITAT** Widespread throughout northern Europe in bushes and low plants, and on the ground.

**FOOD AND HABITS** Seen spring and summer. Hunts by lying in wait on flowers and pouncing on insect prey. Well camouflaged.

# Daddy-long-legs Spider
*Pholcus phalangioides*

**Size and description** Length 7–10mm. Cylindrical abdomen and very long legs, reaching 40mm in length. Pale yellowish-grey in colour.
**Habitat** Inhabits rooms and cellars in buildings, and also caves, across central and southern Europe.
**Food and habits** Female seen year round, male only spring–summer. Hangs upside-down from a flimsy web in which it catches flies and other spiders. Prey is trapped by having thread spun over it. When disturbed, the spider vibrates rapidly and spins to confuse predators.

# Common Harvestman
*Phalangium opilio*

Length 5–8mm. Greyish or yellowish with a pure white underside. Legs are very long and thin. Female is slightly larger than male. Found anywhere in Europe that has dense vegetation. Nocturnal feeder on other small invertebrates. Overwinters as an egg and matures in late summer.

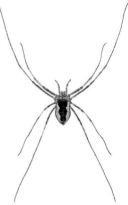

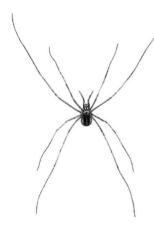

# Harvestman
*Opilio parietinus*

Length 5–9mm. A brown or greyish harvestman with darker bands and sometimes a pale stripe down the back. Female may have a saddle-like mark on her back. Underside is off-white with brown spots. Brown legs are long and hair-like. Found on tree trunks, bushes and rough grasses across Europe except far north. Especially common around human habitation. Feeds on small invertebrates. Often seen on walls and fences.

# European Harvestman

*Leiobunum rotundum*

SIZE AND DESCRIPTION Length to 7mm (f), 4mm (m). Female has an oval pale brown body with an almost rectangular patch on the back. Male has a rusty-brown circular body with a black eye-turret on the back. Legs are long and very thin. Length of second leg can reach 5cm. Female is almost twice as large as male. One of 23 British harvestman species.

HABITAT Dense vegetation throughout most of Europe except far north and far south.

FOOD AND HABITS Feeds on small invertebrates. Often seen resting by day on walls and tree trunks. Harvestmen differ from spiders in lacking poison glands, being unable to produce silk and having a single button-like body.

# Harvestman
*Nemastoma bimaculatum*

**SIZE AND DESCRIPTION** Length 2.5mm. A harvestman that has a small and rotund body with relatively short legs compared with other harvestman species. Mainly black in colour with two white to pale yellow patches behind the head.

**HABITAT** Moss and vegetable debris in shaded habitats such as woods and hedgerows. Occurs in most of Europe.

**FOOD AND HABITS** Found throughout the year. Predates on small creatures that it can overpower.

# Common Newt
*Triturus vulgaris*

**SIZE AND DESCRIPTION** Length 7–11cm. Breeding male develops a wavy crest along the neck, back and tail, and has a bright orange belly with black spots. Smaller female is less clearly marked, lacks a crest and has a paler belly.

**HABITAT** Damp places in many habitats. Found across Europe except far north and far south.

**FOOD AND HABITS** Eats insects, caterpillars, crustaceans, molluscs, worms, tadpoles and slugs. Adults enter the water February–March, leaving it June–July to hibernate in October. Pairs perform complex displays in the water. Lifespan up to 20 years.

# Crested Newt
*Triturus cristatus*

SIZE AND DESCRIPTION Length 11–16cm. Large, colourful and warty. Upper part dark brown or slaty-black. Underside bright orange-yellow spotted with black. Breeding males develop a ragged crest along the back and another on the tail.

HABITAT Breeds in lowland water bodies such as clay pits, reservoirs, ditches and ponds, preferring pools 30–100cm deep. Occurs throughout Europe except Ireland, Iberia and northern Scandinavia.

FOOD AND HABITS Hunts invertebrates and frog tadpoles at night. Enters the water mid-March, and remains until July–August. Hibernation begins October. Eggs are laid on leaves. Larvae metamorphose in four months, and adults are sexually mature at three years. Lifespan up to 27 years.

Female

Male

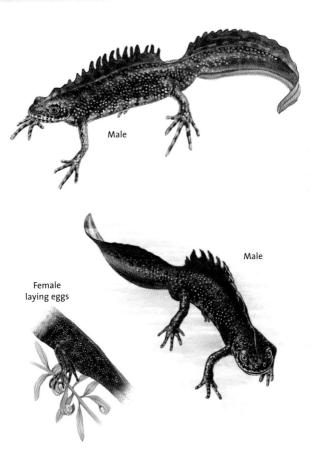

Male

Male

Female
laying eggs

# Common Toad
*Bufo bufo*

**SIZE AND DESCRIPTION** Length 8–15cm. Skin warty and usually orange-brown or olive. Female is larger than male. Walks and hops.

**HABITAT** Lives in a range of habitats, but usually found in damp places. Absent from Ireland, northern Scandinavia and the Mediterranean islands.

**FOOD AND HABITS** Insects, larvae, spiders, worms and slugs are grabbed by the long and sticky, prehensile tongue. Emerges from hibernation to enter water February–March. Hibernates again in October. Male clings to female's back and fertilizes the ribbons of 600–4,000 eggs as she releases them. Toadlets leave pond late July–August. Lifespan up to 40 years.

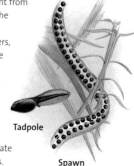

Tadpole

Spawn

# Edible Frog
## *Rana esculenta*

**SIZE AND DESCRIPTION** Length to 11cm. Colour ranges from mainly green to mainly brown. Generally a number of dark spots on the back and flanks, with long back legs often having dark bands. Usually a straw-yellow or lime-green line running along the centre of the back. Underside mottled pale white to yellow and black.

**HABITAT** Highly aquatic and occurs in a variety of waterways. Widespread across much of mainland Europe. Naturalized in Britain.

**FOOD AND HABITS** Very active during the day; enjoys basking even in the hottest sun. Tadpoles can grow very large (up to 4cm), because they overwinter, metamorphosing into frogs the following spring.

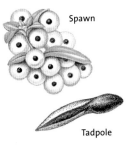

Spawn

Tadpole

# Common Frog
*Rana temporaria*

SIZE AND DESCRIPTION  Length 6–8cm. Smoother skin and longer hindlegs
than Common Toad (page 122). Hindlegs are short compared with
those of other frogs. Colour and pattern vary. Snout is rounded and
the large black eyes are surrounded by gold flecked with brown.
Moves with a springing leap.

HABITAT  Widespread in moist shady habitats, from northern Spain
to the North Cape. Absent from Iceland, Orkney and Shetland.

FOOD AND HABITS  Snails, slugs, worms, woodlice, beetles and flies are
flicked into the wide mouth by its long tongue. Hibernates in pond
mud or rotting vegetation on land. Lays up to 1,400 eggs. Tadpoles
metamorphose into froglets in 12 weeks, and they stay near water
until hibernating October–November. Sexually mature in three years.
Lifespan up to eight years.

**Diet includes animals
that may be harmful to
garden plants, such as
slugs and snails**

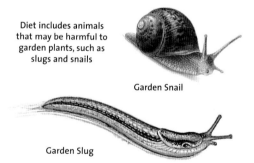

Garden Snail

Garden Slug

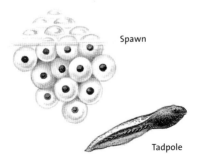

Spawn

Tadpole

# Viviparous Lizard
*Lacerta vivipara*

**SIZE AND DESCRIPTION** Length 10–16cm. Tail may be twice the body length. Skin has obvious scales and a variable pattern. Female usually has a stripe down the middle of her back. Pale spots on the back are more obvious in male than female. Pale underside is orange in some males.

**HABITAT** Occurs across Europe to the Alps and northern Spain. In south lives in damp places at up to about 3,000m; in north occurs in open areas such as overgrown and secluded gardens.

**FOOD AND HABITS** Hunts by day using sight and scent. Prey includes spiders, insects and small snails. Hibernates October–March. Young develop in thin membranous eggs inside female's body. Eggs are laid June–September, with young 'hatching' immediately. Lifespan up to 12 years.

# Common Wall Lizard
*Podarcis muralis*

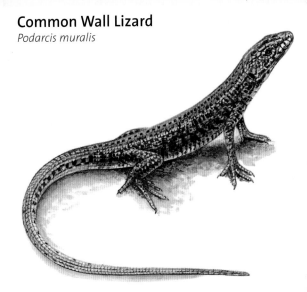

**SIZE AND DESCRIPTION** Length 18–20cm. Tail can be more than twice the body length. Longer and more pointed head than Viviparous Lizard's (opposite). Colours vary from brownish or greyish to greenish.

**HABITAT** Found on walls and tree trunks. Occurs from northern Spain, across France and Italy, to the Balkans and Greece.

**FOOD AND HABITS** Feeds on small invertebrates. Lives in colonies. Hibernates November–February, except in warmer places. The 2–10 eggs are laid in a hole dug in the ground, and hatch July–September. Lifespan up to seven years.

# Slow-worm
*Anguis fragilis*

**Size and description** Length 30–52cm. A legless lizard with a round head and smooth-scaled body. Brownish, but blue may show on older individuals.

**Habitat** Meadows, woodland margins, gardens and cemeteries, from Britain and western Spain to Russia and southern Scandinavia.

**Food and habits** Hunts slow-moving invertebrates, usually early in the morning or in the evening. Mating takes place April–June. The 6–12 young develop inside female for 3–5 months, before being born August–September. Lifespan up to 50 years.

# Grass Snake
*Natrix natrix*

SIZE AND DESCRIPTION Length 70–150cm. Slender pale snake with a distinct head and dark marks on either side of its neck. Mouth looks curved. Female is bigger than male.

HABITAT Lowland hedgerows, woodland margins, heaths, moorland, water meadows, gravel pits and gardens. Found in England and Wales across continental Europe, except far north and far south.

FOOD AND HABITS Eats frogs, fish, tadpoles, newts, mice, voles and birds. Swims well. Hibernates October–March in holes, crevices and manure heaps. Mating takes place April–May; 8–40 eggs are laid June–early August in manure heaps, haystacks, compost heaps or rotting logs. Eggs hatch August–September. Lifespan up to 25 years.

# European Adder
*Viper berus*

SIZE AND DESCRIPTION Length 55–90cm. Colour variable, ranging from light with small and incomplete dark dorsal cross-bars, to entirely dark in melanistic individuals. Head usually with a distinctive V or X on the back. Dark streak from eye to neck continues as a series of spots along the flanks. Female usually brownish with dark brown markings, male pure grey with black markings.

HABITAT Includes chalky downs, moors, rocky hillsides, meadows, rough commons, hedgerows, dumps and large gardens, in much of Europe.

FOOD AND HABITS Timid, biting only when cornered or alarmed – may hiss loudly to warn off aggressors. Bites not highly dangerous to humans. Feeds mainly on small mammals and reptiles. Young, numbering 3–20, born August–September. Hibernates in winter. Lifespan 10–15 years.

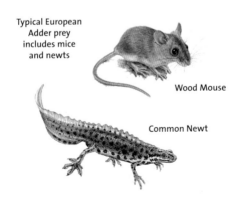

Typical European Adder prey includes mice and newts

Wood Mouse

Common Newt

Female

Male

# Common Pheasant
*Phasianus colchicus*

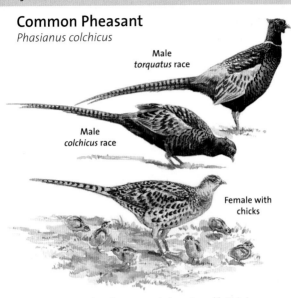

Male *torquatus* race

Male *colchicus* race

Female with chicks

SIZE AND DESCRIPTION Length 75–90cm (m); 53–64cm (f). Male has a long, barred golden tail, a green head and red wattles. Some males have a white ring around the neck. Female has a shorter tail and is buffish-brown.

VOICE A loud, hoarse metallic call, 'koo-krock', usually followed by a whirring wingbeat.

HABITAT Woodlands, farmland with hedges, big gardens and reed beds in much of Europe. Introduced to Greece from Asia 2,000 years ago and has spread across much of Europe.

FOOD AND HABITS Feeds on seeds, fruits, nuts and roots. Male has more than one mate. Nest a grassy cup on the ground.

# Grey Heron
*Ardea cinerea*

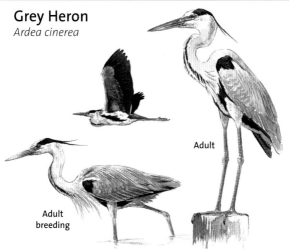

Adult

Adult
breeding

**SIZE AND DESCRIPTION** Length 95cm. Very large and mainly grey bird, with black-and-white markings. Breeding plumage includes long black plumes on the head, a white neck and a yellow bill. Neck is tucked back in flight; wingbeats are slow and ponderous.

**VOICE** Flight call a hoarse croaking 'kraark' and 'chraa'; bill-clapping at the nest.

**HABITAT** Year round in marshes, ponds, lakes, rivers, canals, flooded fields and estuaries throughout Europe except far north. Enters gardens, especially early in the morning, in search of fish.

**FOOD AND HABITS** Feeds on fish, amphibians, small mammals, insects and reptiles. Hunts by stalking slowly through shallow water, or standing motionless waiting for prey to come within reach, when it strikes with lightning speed. Nests in colonies, usually high in tall trees, in huge nest.

# Collared Dove
*Streptopelia decaocto*

**Adult**

**SIZE AND DESCRIPTION** Length 31–33cm. Slimmer than other pigeons.
Back brown-buff, head and underparts pinkish-brown. Black ring
around the neck.

**VOICE** Rapidly repeated 'koo-koo, koo' call.

**HABITAT** Towns, gardens and farmland with hedges. Has spread across
Europe from Asia.

**FOOD AND HABITS** Feeds on seeds and grain, and is a frequent bird-table
visitor. Large flocks assemble at grain stores. Nest a platform of twigs
on a tree branch. Up to five broods a year.

# Woodpigeon
*Columba palumbus*

**Adult**

**Juvenile**

**SIZE AND DESCRIPTION** Length 40–42cm. Adults have white rings around the neck, and a white bar across each wing. Wings make a clattering sound on take-off and landing.

**VOICE** Soft and often repeated 'coo-coo-coo-cu-coo'.

**HABITAT** Woodland, farmland, parks and gardens. Found throughout Europe except far north.

**FOOD AND HABITS** Eats seeds, berries and beechmast. Feeds in flocks in winter. Nest a raft of twigs on a branch. Three broods or more a year.

# Feral Pigeon
*Columba livia*

**SIZE AND DESCRIPTION** Length 31–33cm. Black wing-bars and a white rump. Colours vary from white to very dark grey, and some individuals may be pale fawn.
**VOICE** Soft cooing.
**HABITAT** Sea cliffs, cities, towns and villages.
**FOOD AND HABITS** Feeds on seeds, grain and discarded human food. Breeds throughout the year, but mainly in spring, with 2–3 broods a year.

**Adults**

# House Martin
## *Delichon urbica*

Length 12.5cm. Stubby appearance. Rump white; wings, head and tail dark blue. Voice a harsh twitter that is higher and more drawn-out when agitated. Song a series of formless chirps. Breeds in colonies in towns and villages, and sometimes on cliffs. Arrives in Europe March–April; leaves September–October. Rarely seen on the ground, except when collecting mud for nest-building. Builds a hemispherical nest under eaves with a small entrance hole.

Juvenile

Adult

# Swift
## *Apus apus*

Length 17cm. Long and narrow crescent-shaped wings, torpedo-shaped body and short forked tail. Very short legs. Dark brown plumage with a pale throat. Voice a shrill monotone scream, often uttered by tight flocks flying around buildings. Breeds in towns and villages. Summer visitor to northern Europe, usually May–August. Catches insects in flight. Spends most of its life on the wing. Nests in a hole in a building.

Adult

# Swallow
## *Hirundo rustica*

Adult

**SIZE AND DESCRIPTION** Length 17–22cm, including tail 3–6.5cm. Wings long and pointed; tail deeply forked. Pale cream underparts, dark blue wings and back, and red throat with a blue-black neck band.

**VOICE** Call in flight a high-pitched 'vit-vit'. Song a rapid rattling twitter.

**HABITAT** Breeds in farmyards and small-village gardens with surrounding open country. Often near water. Summer visitor, arriving late March–April, and leaving September–October.

**FOOD AND HABITS** Feeds on insects, which it catches in flight. Nests in outbuildings and porches, on rafters or shelves. Cup nest built from small pieces of mud, lined with grass or straw.

# Great Spotted Woodpecker
*Dendrocopos major*

Male

Female

**SIZE AND DESCRIPTION** Length 23–26cm. Blackbird-sized black-and-white bird. White shoulder patches and red under the tail. Male has a red patch on his nape; female's nape is black. Juvenile has a red crown. Flight is undulating.

**VOICE** Short sharp 'tchak' call, which may be repeated at 1-second intervals. In spring drums very fast on rotten branches.

**HABITAT** All kinds of woodland, large gardens and parks.

**FOOD AND HABITS** Feeds on insects and grubs, and conifer seeds in winter. Visits garden feeders. Also steals eggs and young from other birds' nests. Nests in holes excavated in tree trunks.

# Wren
*Troglodytes troglodytes*

**SIZE AND DESCRIPTION** Length 9–10cm. Tiny brown bird with a short upright tail. Faintly barred reddish-brown back and paler flanks. Narrow dark eye-stripe with a paler stripe above the eye. Bill narrow, pointed and slightly downwards-curving.
**VOICE** Calls a repeated 'tic-tic' and metallic 'clink'. Song a loud series of trills and warbles.
**HABITAT** Woodland with dense undergrowth, scrub, heathland, gardens, parks and moorland.
**FOOD AND HABITS** Searches for insects and spiders on or near the ground, moving in a rather mouse-like fashion. Male builds several nests in his territory. Female selects one, which is then lined with feathers. Nest domed and well camouflaged.

# Dunnock
*Prunella modularis*

Juvenile

Adult

SIZE AND DESCRIPTION Length 13–15cm. Streaking and brown colour give the Dunnock a rather sparrow-like appearance. Thin insect-picking bill, grey throat and face, and reddish-brown legs.

VOICE Alarm call a strong 'tiih'. Song clear and quite loud.

HABITAT Gardens, parks, open woodland, heathland, farmland hedges and young forestry plantations. Resident in most of Europe.

FOOD AND HABITS An unobtrusive bird that searches on the ground for seeds, berries, insects and other invertebrates. Nest built of grass, lined with hair and moss.

# Blackbird
*Turdus merula*

**Female**

SIZE AND DESCRIPTION
Length 23.5–29cm. Male
is all-black with a yellow
bill and yellow eye-ring.
Female and juveniles
are sooty-brown with a
dark-streaked pale throat.

VOICE Alarm call a harsh 'chack-
aack-aack-aack'; also a series of high metallic
notes when going to roost or when a cat
is seen. Rich melodic fluting song, often
rising to a crescendo.

HABITAT Woodland, parks, orchards and
gardens across Europe.

FOOD AND HABITS Takes a wide range of
food, including insects, worms, fruits
and berries. Hops or walks over the
ground, stopping and cocking its head
to look for worms or other food. Nest
made of grasses, with a mud cup
lined with finer grasses.

**Male**

# Mistle Thrush
*Turdus viscivorus*

Length 22–27cm. Upright and comparatively longer tail than Song Thrush's. White breast speckled with rounded blotchy spots. Upright posture on the ground. Flight call a dry churring rattle. Song full-blooded, but similar to Song Thrush's. Breeds in open woodland, orchards, and parks and gardens with trees. Moves into fields and parkland to feed in winter. Eats worms, berries and insects. Nest is built in a tree fork.

# Song Thrush
*Turdus philomelos*

Length 20–22cm. Brown back and speckled creamy breast (speckles shaped like arrowheads). Loud strong song with trilling and squeaky notes; few pauses and frequent repetitions. Alarm call a series of sharp scolding notes. Contact call in flight a fine sharp 'zit'. Found in woodland, parks and gardens. Feeds on worms, insects, berries and snails, the shells of which it smashes on hard ground or rocks. Builds a neat cup-nest of grasses and fine twigs, lined with mud.

# Redwing
*Turdus iliacus*

SIZE AND DESCRIPTION Length 21cm.
Similar size to Song Thrush (page
143), but with visibly larger head. White
stripe above the eye and a black-tipped
yellow bill give it a striking appearance.
Red patch under the wing is conspicuous
in flight, which is fast and direct.
VOICE Thin 'tseep' contact call on
migration. Alarm call hoarse and
scolding. Song variable, with loud fluted
notes and prolonged twitters.
HABITAT Fields, open woodland, parks and
gardens. Summer visitor to northern Europe,
wintering in southern and western Europe, where it feeds in hedges,
moving to open fields and gardens as hedgerow food runs out.
FOOD AND HABITS Feeds on worms, insects and berries. In gardens
attracted to berry-bearing shrubs (above, right) such as cotoneaster
and pyracantha. Nest a grassy cup in a shrub or tree.

Adult

# Fieldfare
*Turdus pilaris*

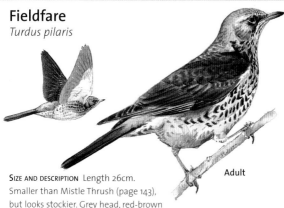

**Adult**

**Size and description** Length 26cm.
Smaller than Mistle Thrush (page 143),
but looks stockier. Grey head, red-brown
back and apricot base to the speckled breast. Longish tail, pale grey
rump and white underwings show in flight. Rather flapping flight.
**Voice** Call a harsh 'chack-chack-chack'. Song a tuneless and
chattering babble.
**Habitat** Open forest, town parks, fields and gardens. Winter visitor or
migrant to much of Europe; year-round in north-central areas;
summer only in far north. In Britain breeds rarely in Scotland.
**Food and habits** Feeds on worms, insects, berries and fruits. Fond of
windfall fruits (below) in gardens and orchards during hard weather.
Nest a grassy cup in a fork of a tree.

# Goldcrest
*Regulus regulus*

Female

Male

Size and description Length 8.5–9.5cm. Greenish back and yellow crest that becomes orange in male. Crest has a black stripe on each side. Face greyish with dark eyes surrounded by very pale grey.

Voice Very high-pitched thin call of 3–4 syllables, 'see-see-see'. Song high-pitched and rhythmic, ending with a trill or flourish.

Habitat Coniferous mixed woodland with spruce and fir preferred. In gardens often seen in Yews and cypress trees.

Food and habits Feeds on tiny insects and spiders on the undersides of leaves and branches. Nest a cup of feathers and moss built high in a tree, often near a branch tip.

# Robin
*Erithacus rubecula*

Adult

Juvenile

**SIZE AND DESCRIPTION**  Length 12.5–14cm. Orange-red breast is fringed
with pale grey, and orange covers the face. Underparts pale; back
brown. Pale wing-bar. Adopts a perky stance.

**VOICE**  Call a short hard repeated 'tic'. Alarm call a thin sharp 'tsiih'.
Song sweet, starting high, followed by a fall, then speeding up in
clear squeaky notes.

**HABITAT**  Woodland bird that breeds in gardens, parks and forest
edges across Europe.

**FOOD AND HABITS**  Feeds on berries and insects on the ground. In winter
will search for food in molehills, animal tracks in snow and where
soil is being turned over by gardeners. Builds a cup nest in a tree
stump, on a branch, among ivy or in an open-fronted nestbox.

# Spotted Flycatcher
*Muscicapa striata*

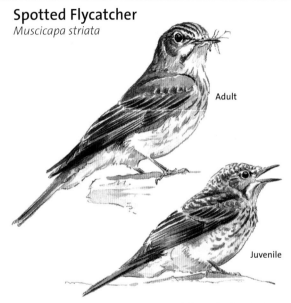

**Adult**

**Juvenile**

**SIZE AND DESCRIPTION** Length 13.5–15cm. Greyish-brown back and pale underparts. Streaked forehead and faintly streaked upper breast. Eyes, bill and legs are black. Perches in an upright posture.

**VOICE** Call a short shrill 'tzee'. Song quiet, simple and scratchy, often with soft trills.

**HABITAT** Open woodland, parks and gardens. Summer visitor to Britain end April–September.

**FOOD AND HABITS** Snatches insects in flight, then returns to the same perch. Builds a cup nest between a branch and tree trunk, among espaliered trees against a wall or in an open-fronted nestbox.

# Long-tailed Tit
*Aegithalos caudatus*

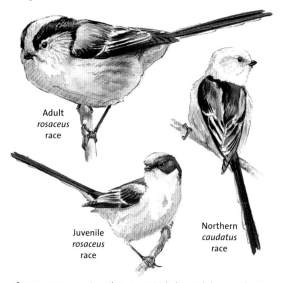

Adult
*rosaceus*
race

Northern
*caudatus*
race

Juvenile
*rosaceus*
race

**SIZE AND DESCRIPTION** Length 12–14cm, including tail that is at least as long as its dumpy body. Unmistakable pink, black and white body, and dark tail.

**VOICE** Piercing, trisyllabic continuous call, 'zee-zee-zee'.

**HABITAT** Woods with bushy undergrowth, hedges and gardens.

**FOOD AND HABITS** Feeds mainly on insects and small spiders, and increasingly visits bird tables. Families form into flocks and move through woods and hedges, often with other tits. Constructs an attractive dome-shaped nest of moss and feathers.

# Great Tit
*Parus major*

**SIZE AND DESCRIPTION** Length
14 cm. Black cap and black stripe
starting at the bill. Male's breast-
stripe becomes broader than female's.

**VOICE** Rich and varied repertoire includes
a metallic 'pink' and 'teacher-teacher'.

**HABITAT** Woodland and gardens
across Europe except far north.

**FOOD AND HABITS** Feeds on seeds
and fruits, and spiders and
insect larvae in breeding season.
Builds a cup nest in a tree hole.

**Female**

**Male**

▼ **SIMILAR SPECIES Coal Tit** (*Periparus ater*). 11.5cm long.
Smaller than Great Tit. Black head, white cheeks and white
patch on nape. British birds have an olive hue to the back plumage,
while continental birds have a blue-grey back; Irish birds have pale
sulphur-yellow cheeks, breast and belly. Most frequent call a triple
'tsee-tsee-tsee'. Song like a weaker Great Tit's song. Inhabits woodland
and gardens across Europe except far north. Prefers coniferous trees.
Eats insects and seeds. Nests in holes in trees.

**British**
*britanicus*
**race**

**Continental**
*ater* **race**

# Blue Tit
*Cyanistes caeruleus*

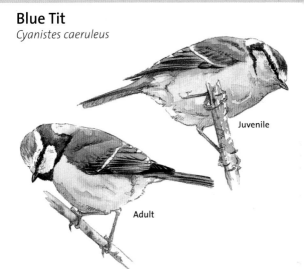

Juvenile

Adult

**Size and description** Length 11–12cm. Smaller than Great Tit (opposite) and with a bright blue crown. Stripe down yellow breast is less well defined. Tail and wings blue.

**Voice** Clear and high-pitched ringing song, and thin 'see-see' call.

**Habitat** Mixed and deciduous woodland, parks and gardens. Found throughout Europe except far north.

**Food and habits** Feeds on insects, spiders and other small animals, finding them on tree branches and sometimes in the corners of windows. Often visits bird tables in winter. Builds a cup nest in a hole in a tree or in a nestbox.

# Nuthatch
*Sitta europaea*

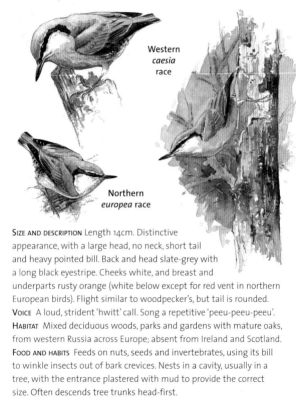

**Western *caesia* race**

**Northern *europea* race**

**SIZE AND DESCRIPTION** Length 14cm. Distinctive appearance, with a large head, no neck, short tail and heavy pointed bill. Back and head slate-grey with a long black eyestripe. Cheeks white, and breast and underparts rusty orange (white below except for red vent in northern European birds). Flight similar to woodpecker's, but tail is rounded.

**VOICE** A loud, strident 'hwitt' call. Song a repetitive 'peeu-peeu-peeu'.

**HABITAT** Mixed deciduous woods, parks and gardens with mature oaks, from western Russia across Europe; absent from Ireland and Scotland.

**FOOD AND HABITS** Feeds on nuts, seeds and invertebrates, using its bill to winkle insects out of bark crevices. Nests in a cavity, usually in a tree, with the entrance plastered with mud to provide the correct size. Often descends tree trunks head-first.

# Magpie
*Pica pica*

Adult

**SIZE AND DESCRIPTION** Length 40–51cm, including 20–30cm tail. Wings metallic blue-black, and round-tipped tail has a metallic green sheen. Male larger and tends to have a longer tail than female.

**VOICE** Noisy alarm call is a staccato rattle. Also various bisyllabic calls.

**HABITAT** Breeds around farms and villages, and in hedgerows. Increasingly common in urban areas. Occurs throughout Europe except Iceland and northernmost Scotland.

**FOOD AND HABITS** Omnivore that feeds on seeds, insects, carrion, nestlings and eggs. Nest a football-sized twig dome built in a tree or large hedge.

# Carrion Crow
*Corvus corone*

**SIZE AND DESCRIPTION** Length
44–51cm. Black crow with
a stout bill.

**VOICE** Hard 'krra-kra-kraa'
is the most common call.

**HABITAT** Wide variety of
habitats, from coasts to
mountains and towns, across
western and central Europe.

**FOOD AND HABITS** Omnivorous,
feeding on carrion, nestlings
and eggs, grain and insects.
Builds a large cup nest of twigs and sticks in a tree,
or on a cliff or building.

▶ **SIMILAR SPECIES** **Hooded Crow** (*C. cornis*). Like Carrion
Crow, but with grey underparts and back; also
similar voice and habits. Replaces Carrion
Crow in eastern and northern
Europe. In Britain common in
north-west Scotland
and Ireland; rare
on east coast of
England.

# Jackdaw
*Corvus monedula*

**SIZE AND DESCRIPTION**
Length 30–34cm.
Smallest of
the 'black' crows,
it is not entirely black.
Nape is grey and eye has a
very pale iris. Struts as it walks.

**VOICE** Most common calls a metallic
high-pitched 'kya' and 'chak'.

**HABITAT** Found across Europe on
coasts, in ancient woodland and
near human habitation.

**FOOD AND HABITS** An omnivore,
eating invertebrates, eggs and
nestlings of other birds, small
mammals and grain. Also forages on
rubbish tips, and may feed alongside
other corvids in fields. Natural nest sites
are cavities in old trees (right) or holes in
cliffs and rock faces. Buildings provide
equally acceptable sites, and birds may
nest in chimneys, churches and ruins.

# Jay
*Garrulus glandarius*

**Adult**

**SIZE AND DESCRIPTION** Length 32–35cm. Pinkish-brown body contrasts with the white rump and black tail. Streaked feathers on forehead are often raised in a crest. Pale eye, black moustache and blue-and-black wing-flash.

**VOICE** Call a noisy and screeching 'kscharch'.

**HABITAT** Found in all types of woods, preferring those with a plentiful supply of acorns. Has taken to gardens in some suburban areas. Found across Europe, where it is mostly resident.

**FOOD AND HABITS** Feeds on seeds, fruits, and eggs and nestlings of other birds. Buries acorns, beechnuts and hornbeam seeds for later use. Builds a flat nest of twigs in a tree.

# Starling
*Sturnus vulgaris*

SIZE AND DESCRIPTION Length
19–22cm. Short tail and
neck, upright stance,
pink legs, white spots
and metallic green
sheen. Tends to
be seen in large
numbers, which fly
in tight formation –
the swirling flocks
of thousands of birds
at winter roosts can
be dramatic.

Adult

VOICE A versatile mimic of other birds, but its own calls are creaky
twitters, chirps, clicks and whistles. Alarm call a sharp 'kyett'.

HABITAT Naturally a bird of oak woodland, it has spread into a number
of habitats and seems particularly fond of human settlements.

FOOD AND HABITS Eats a wide variety of food. In winter large flocks
forage in fields and gardens, as well as on seashores. Nests in holes
in buildings, in trees and on cliffs.

Juvenile

# Common Chiffchaff
*Phylloscopus collybita*

**Adult
*collybita*
race**

**Northern
*abietinus*
race**

**SIZE AND DESCRIPTION** Length
10–12cm. Small neat bird
with a fine bill and thin dark
legs. Stripe above the eye,
and a darkish patch
beneath the eye
emphasizing white
eye-ring. Habit of flicking its tail downwards.
**VOICE** Call a soft 'hueet'. Song a slow and
measured 'chiff-chaff-chiff-chaff'.
**HABITAT** Usually breeds in open deciduous woodland with some scrub.
Mainly a summer visitor to Britain, Scandinavia and central Europe,
from mid-March to August–November. Most likely to be seen in
gardens while in transit.
**FOOD AND HABITS** Feeds on small insects, which it finds by flitting
around among foliage. Eats berries in autumn. Builds a domed nest
on the ground.

# House Sparrow
*Passer domesticus*

**Female**

**Male**

**SIZE AND DESCRIPTION** Length 14–16cm. Male has a grey cap and grey breast, with an extensive black throat patch. Brown back with dark streaks in both sexes. Female has a pale brown cap and buff eye-stripe. Wings of both sexes have small white wing-bars.

**VOICE** Various monotonous chirps.

**HABITAT** Found in towns, villages and farmland near human habitation. In winter flocks may feed in fields. Occurs across Europe except far north; declining in Britain.

**FOOD AND HABITS** Omnivorous, feeding on seeds and insects, as well as bread and other food left by people. Social even when breeding. Builds an untidy nest in a hole in a buildings or sometimes a tree.

# Goldfinch
## *Carduelis carduelis*

**SIZE AND DESCRIPTION** Length
12–13.5cm. Striking red face,
white cheeks and throat, black
cap and black-and-gold wings.
Sexes are alike, but juvenile
has a brown-streaked head
until the late summer or
early autumn.

**VOICE** A piercing and cheerful
trisyllabic 'tickelitt' call. Song
rather soft with a series of
rapid trills and twitters
involving the 'tickelitt' call.

**HABITAT** Breeds in open
lowland woodland, heaths,
orchards and gardens, south
from southern Scandinavia.

**FOOD AND HABITS** Feeds on
seeds and berries, taking
insects when feeding young.
Pointed bill enables it to
extract seeds from thistle-
heads and teasels. Nest a
neat structure of grass, moss
and lichens, lined with
thistledown or wool and
built at the tips of branches.

Adult

# Greenfinch
*Carduelis chloris*

Male

Female

**SIZE AND DESCRIPTION** Length 14–16cm. Stouter than most other finches. In summer adults are olive-green, merging into grey-green on the face, wings and flanks, with bright yellow wing feathers on either side of the tail. Female's colouring is subdued, with faint brownish streaks on the back.

**VOICE** Flight call a sharp 'burrurrup'. Song a wheezy sequence of twitters and whistles.

**HABITAT** Breeds in woodland edges, open woodland, parks, gardens and farmland with hedges. In winter flocks may feed in gardens.

**FOOD AND HABITS** Eats seeds and berries, and some insects during the breeding season. A visitor to garden bird tables, where it has acquired a taste for peanuts.

# Chaffinch
*Fringilla coelebs*

Male

Female

**SIZE AND DESCRIPTION** Length 14–16cm. Bright colours of male in spring make it hard to confuse with other species. In winter the blue-grey of the head and pink of the breast are subdued. Female similar to female House Sparrow (page 159).

**VOICE** Call a sharp 'pink', but flight call a softer 'yupp'. Song a loud ringing trill that becomes lower and ends in a flourish, before being repeated again.

**HABITAT** Breeds in all types of woodland, as well as in parks and gardens. British birds are resident, but those from elsewhere in Europe may winter in Britain.

**FOOD AND HABITS** Eats fruits and seeds, and also insects during the breeding season. Nest a neat cup of moss and lichens, lined with feathers and built in the fork of a branch in a small tree or bush.

# Siskin
*Carduelis spinus*

Male

Female

**SIZE AND DESCRIPTION** Length 12cm. Dark-streaked, greenish-yellow plumage. Male yellower than female, with a black cap and bib. Wingbars in both sexes are yellow, and male's tail has yellow patches on either side. Tail is deeply notched. Flight flitting and uneven.
**VOICE** Flight call either a descending 'tilu' or a rising 'tlui'; twittery, trilling song.
**HABITAT** Coniferous and mixed forests in winter in much of Europe.
**FOOD AND HABITS** Seeds of trees, favouring birch and alder catkins, and spruce cones. Nest a cup of twigs high up in tree, usually a conifer. Moves around in flocks in winter.

# Red Squirrel
*Sciurus vulgaris*

SIZE AND DESCRIPTION Length 21–25cm (body); 14–20cm (tail). Several colour morphs ranging from red to black. In winter fur becomes greyer and ear-tufts are prominent. Smaller than Grey Squirrel (page 166).

HABITAT Forests, especially coniferous, and woods dominated by beeches, across much of Europe. Increasingly scarce in Britain, where the main threats to it are an increase in Grey Squirrels, disease (squirrel poxvirus transmitted via Grey Squirrels, which are largely immune) and road traffic.

FOOD AND HABITS Solitary and diurnal, with peaks of activity around dawn and dusk. Feeds mostly on conifer seeds, favouring pine cones, as well as larch and spruce. Also eats fungi, shoots and fruits, and sometimes birds' eggs. Hoards food. Mating varies between winter and spring, according to availability of food and geographical distribution. Nests in dreys, often in the forks of tree trunks. Litter size 3–8. Lifespan 3–5 years, but many die in the first year.

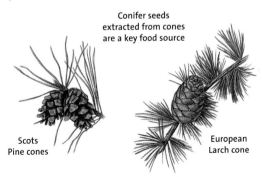

**Conifer seeds extracted from cones are a key food source**

Scots Pine cones

European Larch cone

Pale morph

Dark morph

# Grey Squirrel
*Sciurus carolinensis*

SIZE AND DESCRIPTION Length
23–30cm (body); 19–24cm (tail).
Grey fur is variably tinged
with red and yellow. Some
individuals are noticeably
red in summer.

HABITAT North American species
that has been introduced to
Britain and Ireland, where it is
now very common in wooded
habitats, including gardens
and parks.

FOOD AND HABITS Active during
the day. In summer foraging
takes place mainly in trees, but
it also searches on the ground
for fungi, bulbs, roots and
cached acorns. Food includes
eggs, nestlings, leaves, buds
and shoots. Drey is a large
structure of twigs, leaves, bark
and grass. Does not hibernate.
Breeds May and December. Up
to seven young are born.
Lifespan up to nine years.

Courtship display

Sign of a squirrel's
presence: nutshell
split open

# Edible Dormouse
*Glis glis*

**Sign of a dormouse's presence: smooth-edged hole in nutshell**

**SIZE AND DESCRIPTION** Length 13–19cm (body); 11–15cm (tail). Uniformly grey with a faint yellowish tinge, fleshy nose and naked rounded ears. Eyes are surrounded by dark rings. Bushy tail.

**HABITAT** Mature woodlands, parks and large gardens. Found throughout Europe, but absent from Scandinavia. Introduced to Britain in antiquity.

**FOOD AND HABITS** Nocturnal and secretive, spending the day hidden in a hole in a tree or in an old bird's nest. Forages in the tree canopy; also enters sheds and lofts in search of food. Favours nuts and berries, but some insects and nestlings are also eaten. Hibernation begins October. Breeds June–August. Litter size 4–6. Lifespan up to six years.

# Field Vole
*Microtus agrestis*

**Size and description** Length 9.5–13.5cm (body); 2.5–4.6 cm (tail). Coarse yellowish grey-brown fur and a short tail. Ears are hidden by fur.

**Habitat** Prefers rough grassland and scrub. Also found in open woodland, field margins and hedges. Occurs across Europe from northern Spain; absent from Iceland, Ireland, Italy, the Balkans, Norway and Sweden.

**Food and habits** Mostly nocturnal; sometimes active during the day, particularly in winter. Mainly vegetarian, eating leaves and seeds. Breeds March–October; longer in mild winters. Litter size 2–7, with up to seven litters a year. Only a few voles reach 18 months.

# Bank Vole
*Clethrionomys glareolus*

**Sign of a vole's presence: clearly delineated gnawed edge in nutshell**

SIZE AND DESCRIPTION Length 8–11cm (body); 3.5–7.2cm (tail). Rounded face and small eyes. Bright chestnut fur on the back and buffish-grey underparts.

HABITAT Mixed deciduous woodland with well-developed undergrowth, but also coniferous woodland, grassland and scrub. Occurs across Europe from northern Spain to northern Scandinavia; absent from much of Ireland, Iceland, Italy and Greece.

FOOD AND HABITS Actively searches for seeds, roots, nuts, shoots and buds during the day in summer, with peaks of activity around dawn and dusk. Breeds April–December. Litter size 3–5, with 4–5 litters a year. Lifespan rarely exceeds 18 months.

# Wood Mouse
*Apodemus sylvaticus*

Sign of a mouse's presence: upper teeth marks evident in nutshell

**SIZE AND DESCRIPTION** Length 8–10cm (body); 6.9–11.5cm (tail). Orange-brown fur, noticeable ears and tail that may be longer than the body. Underparts pale grey.

**HABITAT** Every habitat except those that are too wet or too high (above 2,500m). Rare in coniferous woodland. Occurs throughout Europe except far north.

**FOOD AND HABITS** Forages largely at night for seeds, buds, fruits, nuts, snails and spiders. A good climber; can be found in trees and enters houses in search of food. Does not hibernate, but slows down in cold weather. Litter size 2–11, with about six litters a year. Life expectancy 10–17 weeks, but a few reach two years.

# House Mouse
*Mus domesticus*

**SIZE AND DESCRIPTION** Length 7–10cm (body); 6.5–10cm (tail). Uniformly greyish fur, and a thick scaly tail. Colour varies. Emits a strong musky smell when disturbed.

**HABITAT** Originated in rocky habitats in Asia, and now closely associated with humans. Found in buildings and on farmland throughout Europe except far north.

**FOOD AND HABITS** Primarily a grain eater feeding on wide variety of seeds, roots, fungi and invertebrates, taking an average of about 3.5g a day. Litter size 5–8, with 5–10 litters a year. Mortality high, with very few surviving to reach two years.

# Yellow-necked Mouse
*Apodemus flavicollis*

**SIZE AND DESCRIPTION** Length 8.5–13cm (body); 9–13.5cm (tail). Larger, brighter and redder than Wood Mouse (page 171), with a clearer demarcation between the upperside and underside. Distinct yellow bib between the front legs in northern Europe; this is less distinct in the southern area of its range.

**HABITAT** Favours deciduous woodland, wooded gardens and established orchards; also coniferous forests and mountains at up to 2,250m. Occurs in Wales, southern England, northern Spain and France, but not far north.

**FOOD AND HABITS** Eats acorns, seeds, grain, fungi, berries, leaves, insect larvae and pupae, snails and birds' eggs. Hoards food throughout the year. Largely nocturnal. Litter size 2–11, with 3–4 litters a year. Lifespan up to four years.

# Brown Rat
*Rattus norvegicus*

**SIZE AND DESCRIPTION** Length 11–29cm (body); 8.5–23cm (tail). Coarse grey-brown fur and a thick scaly tail.

**HABITAT** Found across Europe except Arctic Scandinavia, in all habitats associated with humans. May move onto farmland in summer in search of cereals.

**FOOD AND HABITS** Wary nocturnal rodent rarely seen by humans, despite living close to them. Prefers grain, but will eat a variety of foods including roots, buds, fruits, frogs, birds' eggs and human refuse. Breeds throughout the year. Litter size 7–8, with about five litters a year. Lifespan one year.

# European Rabbit
*Oryctolagus cuniculus*

**SIZE AND DESCRIPTION** Length 34–50cm (body); 4–8cm (tail). Grey-brown with an off-white belly and long rounded ears. Prominent eyes are chestnut and nose is gently rounded. Underside of the tail is white.
**HABITAT** Favours heathland, meadows, grassland, farmland, woodland and large gardens. Found throughout Europe.
**FOOD AND HABITS** Generally seen around dusk and dawn, or at night. Vegetarian diet includes crops, cereals, saplings, grasses and bulbs. Breeds year round.

# European Hedgehog
*Erinaceus europaeus*

**SIZE AND DESCRIPTION** Length 20–30cm (body); 1–4cm (tail). Rounded short body covered with spines, which are dark with creamy tips. Face and underside are covered with coarse hairs. Longish legs. Pointed nose, small ears and eyes, and pointed teeth.

**HABITAT** Lowlands up to 2,000m, where there is ground cover for shelter and nesting, across Europe except far north.

**FOOD AND HABITS** Eats invertebrates found at ground level, including slugs, worms and beetles, as well as birds' eggs and nestlings, and carrion. Usually nocturnal. Runs quite fast, can climb banks and walls, and swims. Mainly solitary. Spines protect it from most predators. Cars, lawnmowers and poisoning by chemicals such as slug pellets are the main causes of death. Hibernates October–March/April. Litter size 2–7, with 1–2 litters a year. Mortality is high in the first year, but survivors live for about three years.

# European Mole
*Talpa europaea*

**SIZE AND DESCRIPTION** Length 11–16cm (body); 2–4cm (tail). Soft grey-black fur, cylindrical shape, massive earth-moving front paws, tiny eyes covered by fur and a pink bewhiskered nose. Rarely seen above the ground; the hills it leaves on the ground are a sign of its presence.

**HABITAT** Woodland species that has adapted to fields, parks and gardens. Absent from far north and far south.

**FOOD AND HABITS** Active beneath the ground day and night all year. Tunnels may be 1m deep and 200m long. Food is earthworms and insect larvae, which are found by smell and hearing. Female builds a nest of dry grass and leaves, in which she gives birth to 3–4 young. Lifespan about three years.

# Common Shrew
*Sorex araneus*

**SIZE AND DESCRIPTION** Length 5.2–8.7cm (body); 2.4–4.4cm (tail). Adult has a three-coloured coat, consisting of a dark brown head and back, pale brown flanks and grey-brown underparts.

**HABITAT** Widespread in habitats with ground cover, but most common in rough grassland, scrub, woodland and hedges. Found throughout Europe from Scandinavia to Wales, but not in Iceland, Ireland and the Iberian Peninsula.

**FOOD AND HABITS** Active day and night. Uses its long nose to sniff out beetles, spiders, small snails and other invertebrates. Litter size 4–10, with up to five litters a season. Less than 30 per cent survive long enough to breed the following year, and few of these survive until the next breeding season.

# Pygmy Shrew
*Sorex minutus*

**SIZE AND DESCRIPTION** Length 4–6.4cm (body); 3.2–4.6cm (tail). Back and head grey-brown and underside greyish-white. Head more bulbous, and tail thicker and hairier, than Common Shrew's (opposite).
**HABITAT** Similar habitat to Common Shrew. Found in gardens, particularly near compost heaps.
**FOOD AND HABITS** Very agile, often climbing in search of food. Does not burrow itself, but uses burrows of other small mammals, and may dig through leaf litter and surface vegetation. Feeds on insects and other invertebrates 2–6mm long. Eats one-and-a-quarter times its own weight each day. Litter size 4–7, with several litters a season. Lives up to 13 months, but at least half do not survive the first two months.

# Pipistrelle
*Pipistrellus pipistrellus*

**SIZE AND DESCRIPTION** Length 3.5–4.9cm; wingspan 27–30cm. Very small bat with a soft reddish coat, though the colour may vary. Rounded head with small triangular ears. Fast and jerky flight.

**HABITAT** Found across Europe except far north, in all but the most exposed habitats.

**FOOD AND HABITS** In summer roosts in buildings, squeezing through tiny gaps to gain entrance. In winter uses buildings and natural sites for hibernation; also behind boards attached to walls and in specially made boxes. Usually emerges after sunset, but may be seen during daylight. Hunts flying insects for up to 3 hours in warm weather, up to 15 minutes in cold. Each male has a group of 8–10 females. Usually one young is born in spring. Average lifespan four years.

# Brown Long-eared Bat
*Plecotus auritus*

**SIZE AND DESCRIPTION** Length 3–4.3cm; wingspan 23–28.5cm. Not a large bat, but with prominent ears that are clearly visible in flight. Fluffy fur is greyish-brown with a paler underside. Brown wings are translucent.

**HABITAT** Found in mature woodland, parkland and large gardens at up to 2,000m. Absent from Spain, Iceland and northern Scandinavia.

**FOOD AND HABITS** Summer roosts with up to 60 individuals are in old trees, buildings and bat boxes. Winter roosts are in caves, tunnels and disused mines. May move to a new roost in trees in mid-winter. Hibernates late October–early April. Litter size 1–2 , born mid-June– July. Average lifespan four and a half years.

# Noctule
*Nyctalus noctula*

**Size and description** Length 3–8cm; wingspan 32–40cm. Almost twice the size of Pipistrelle (page 180), with narrow wings. Coat golden-brown, but moults into a duller paler brown in August–September. Wings are dark brown or black.

**Habitat** Lowland deciduous woodland, parkland and gardens with mature trees. Absent from Iceland, Scotland and far north.

**Food and habits** Uses tree-holes as summer roosts; also bat boxes. In winter roosts in trees and buildings. Emerges from roosts at dusk. Catches and eats flying insects on the wing. Offspring born June–July; usually only one young is produced. May live for 12 years, but most die much sooner.

# Red Fox
*Vulpes vulpes*

**SIZE AND DESCRIPTION** Length 56–77cm (body); 28–49cm (tail); 35–40cm (height at shoulder). Pointed nose and ears, and bushy tail, make this reddish-brown carnivore unmistakable.

**HABITAT** Found in every type of habitat, including urban areas, at up to 3,500m in mountains. Widespread across Europe except Iceland.

**FOOD AND HABITS** Active mostly at night with peak activity at dawn and dusk. Preys on small mammals and birds, but about two-thirds of an urban fox's diet is human refuse. Also eats carrion, as well as hedgerow berries and fruits. Lives in family groups. Litter size 4–5 cubs, which are born black. Some foxes survive for 12 years, but most live for only about two.

# Eurasian Badger
*Meles meles*

**SIZE AND DESCRIPTION** Length 67–85cm (body); 11–20cm (tail); 30cm (height at shoulder). Black stripe through each eye, a white face and coarse greyish fur. Although the sexes are alike, male has a broad domed head, while female's head is narrower and flatter, and she has a bushier tail.

**HABITAT** Deciduous woodland with open areas or bordering farmland; also parks, gardens and mountains up to 2,000m. Occurs in most of Europe except far northern.

**FOOD AND HABITS** Eats earthworms, small mammals, birds, eggs, reptiles and frogs; also berries, fruits, roots and honey, and grubs in wasps' and bees' nests. Most cubs born January–March. Litter consists of 1–5 cubs. If they survive their first year, badgers live for about six years.

# Pine Marten
*Martes martes*

**SIZE AND DESCRIPTION** Length 40–55cm (body); 22–26cm (tail). Flattened head, long neck and short legs. Fur predominantly dark brown, but throat is cream or pale yellow.

**HABITAT** Woodland, particularly coniferous forests, at up to 2,000m. Moves into lofts and farm buildings in winter. Found across Europe from northern Spain. In Britain limited to north of Scotland, the Lake District, north Wales, Yorkshire and western Ireland.

**FOOD AND HABITS** Nocturnal. Good climber and jumper. Feeds on small mammals, birds' eggs and nestlings. Also eats berries, fruits and wild bees' honey. Usually three young are born March–April. If the first winter is survived, life expectancy is about five years.

# Weasel
*Mustela nivalis*

**Size and description** Length 13–23cm (body); 3–6cm (tail). Long body and neck. Fur chestnut-brown with white underparts. Male much larger than female.

**Habitat** Found in lowland woods, farmland and large gardens across Europe, except Ireland and Iceland.

**Food and habits** Hunts day and night, with three periods of sleep (3–4 hours each) every day. Prey is mainly voles, but also young rabbits, rats, moles and nestlings. Cannot survive more than 24 hours without food. Solitary outside breeding season. Litter size 3–8. Life expectancy about a year in the wild.

# Stoat
*Mustela erminea*

**SIZE AND DESCRIPTION** Length 24–31cm (body); 9–14cm (tail). Larger than Weasel (opposite), with more reddish-brown fur and a black-tipped tail. In the north of its range in winter, its coat turns clean white except for the tail tip, which remains black. Male larger than female.

**HABITAT** Wide range of habitats, wherever there is suitable food. Occurs across Europe except lowlands around Mediterranean and Iceland.

**FOOD AND HABITS** Moves with a bounding gait and is a good swimmer and agile climber. Hunts by day and night either singly or in family parties. Prey includes small mammals and birds. Mates in summer, but gestation, of 21–28 days, is delayed until the following spring, when a litter of 6–12 is born. Life expectancy 1–2 years.

# Reeves's Muntjac
*Muntiacus reevesi*

**SIZE AND DESCRIPTION** Length 90–107cm (body); 14–18cm (tail); 44–52cm (height at shoulder). Red-brown deer with a dark V-shape on the head. Buck has short antlers and long incisors, which may protrude from its upper lip. Coat is grey-brown and legs are nearly black in autumn.
**HABITAT** Dense deciduous woodland with thick undergrowth; also gardens and orchards. Introduced to Britain from China in the 1900s; now found in England, Wales and other parts of western Europe.
**FOOD AND HABITS** Eats grass during spring; browses on shrubs and the lower branches of deciduous trees. Normally solitary and active day and night, particularly around dusk and dawn. One fawn is born after a seven-month gestation. Many muntjac die in hard winters; lifespan of survivors is 16 years.

# Roe Deer
*Capreolus capreolus*

**SIZE AND DESCRIPTION** Length 100–140cm (body); 1–2cm (tail); 100–140cm (height at shoulder). Coat reddish-brown in summer, moulting into longer grey-brown to almost black in autumn. Short muzzle with a black nose, and large dark eyes. Bucks have small antlers (to 30cm) with three tines.

**HABITAT** Deciduous and coniferous woodland, open moorland and sometimes reedbeds, across much of Europe. Enters large gardens.

**FOOD AND HABITS** Feeds on the buds and shoots of trees and shrubs, brambles, wild flowers, ivy, ferns and berries. Mostly solitary. May form small flocks in winter; males may be seen with females in breeding season. Rutting July–August. Implantation is delayed and gestation starts December–January. Young (usually twins) born April–June. Most die in the first few months; lifespan of survivors is 12–14 years.

# Index